FLINT IMPLEMENTS

Arma antiqua manus, ungues, dentesque fuerunt
Et lapides, et item silvarum fragmina rami.
Lucretius, De Rerum Natura, V. *1282*

FLINT IMPLEMENTS

an account of stone age techniques and cultures

LONDON   1968

THE TRUSTEES OF THE BRITISH MUSEUM

© 1968, The Trustees of the British Museum

first published 1949
second edition 1956
third edition 1968
[SBN 7141 1306 9]

Made and printed in Great Britain by
William Clowes and Sons, Limited, London and Beccles

PREFACE

This handbook was written in this Department by Mr William Watson, Assistant Keeper, now in the Department of Oriental Antiquities. It is called 'Flint Implements' to establish its relationship to Mr Reginald Smith's popular little book 'Flints', first published in 1926, and the new title must, like 'Flints', be accepted as one of convenience and not as a precisely accurate description of the contents. The present work is, in fact, much more than a revision of 'Flints', over twenty years of research in prehistory having made an altered treatment necessary. There is a fuller account of the dating-methods and cultural classifications of the Stone Age artifacts, subjects upon which all interested persons now ask for information, and the methods of prehistoric enquiry have been clarified by keeping apart the chronological, technological, and cultural aspects of the subject. On the other hand, the illustrations, all but three of specimens in the British Museum collections, are grouped according to types rather than cultural assemblages, thus emphasizing the continual technological progress which was the special theme of 'Flints'. The handbook has been prepared with the knowledge of the Department of Geology in the Natural History Museum, where a complementary guide 'Man the Toolmaker' has been written by Dr Kenneth Oakley.

August 1949
T. D. KENDRICK,
Keeper of British and Medieval Antiquities

PREFACE TO SECOND EDITION

In this second edition the type has been re-set throughout. There is a new section on dating by means of radio-active substances, and a new table on the Pleistocene in South Africa, supplementing the table for East Africa which appeared in the first edition. The opportunity has been taken to make minor amendments and adjustments to the text. The revision has been carried out by the author of the first edition, Mr William Watson, Assistant Keeper in the Department of Oriental Antiquities.

R. L. S. BRUCE-MITFORD,
Keeper of British and
Medieval Antiquities

The British Museum,
February 1956

PREFACE TO THIRD EDITION

This is the third edition of 'Flint Implements', first published by the Trustees in 1949. The basic work is that of Professor William Watson, at one time in the department of British and Medieval Antiquities. This edition has been revised and brought into line with the latest knowledge by Mr G. de G. Sieveking, F.S.A., Assistant Keeper in the Department.

R. L. S. BRUCE-MITFORD,
Keeper of British and
Medieval Antiquities

The British Museum,
November 1967

CONTENTS

Preface	page 5
Preface to Second Edition	5
Preface to Third Edition	6
Prehistory	9
Time	10
The Raw Material	23
Flint	25
The Culture Sequence	37
The Earliest Tools	42
The Clactonian Culture	43
The Chopper Cultures	45
The Acheulean Culture	45
The Levalloisian Technique	53
The Spread from Africa	57
The Mousterian Culture	58
The Blade Technique	61
The Upper Palaeolithic in Western Europe	63
The Early Perigordian Culture	64
The Aurignacian Culture	64
The Perigordian Culture	64
The Solutrean Culture	66
The Magdalenian Culture	67
The Upper Palaeolithic in Britain	68
The Mesolithic of Europe	69
Early Farming Cultures	74
Select Bibliography	79
Plates	81
Index	104
Chronological Tables	110

ILLUSTRATIONS IN TEXT

1. Cones of percussion *page* 27
2. Ideal flake 28
3. Hinge fracture and exaggerated ripples 29
4. Pot-lid fracture and frost-pitting 31
5. Starch fracture 32
6. Clactonian core and flake 44
7. Hand-axe in the making 48
8. Step-flaking 49
9. Outlines of hand-axes 50
10. Levalloisian core and flake 54
11. Mousterian disc core 59
12. Blade cores and rejuvenating flake 62
13. Blade notched for microlith. Microburin 73

PLATES

I. Pebble tools and hand-axes 82
II. Late hand-axes and early flakes 84
III. The prepared-platform flake technique 86
IV. Leaf-shaped knives and points 88
V. Knives, daggers and sickles 90
VI. Scrapers 92
VII. Arrowheads and other projectile points 94
VIII. Burins and microliths 96
IX. Axe-heads used for tree felling 98
X. Perforated stone axes, mace-heads and antler mounting 100
XI. Sickle blades 102

PREHISTORY

The story of mankind is divided into a prehistoric and a historic period, the latter distinguished by the use of writing. The prehistoric period, which is the longer by some fifty times at least, can be investigated only in the light of surviving scraps of human material equipment, and the further back we pursue the story the scantier these scraps become. The oldest traces of human activity are stone tools. The first that attracted serious attention was found in England. Shortly before the year 1690 a pear-shaped flint implement was found near an elephant's skeleton in a gravel-pit opposite Black Mary's, near Grays Inn Lane, London. This was described as a 'British' (i.e. pre-Roman) weapon and is the first stone tool known to have been collected as a specimen of human handiwork. The first person, however, to appreciate the real significance of the association of worked flints with the bones of extinct animals was John Frere, who in 1797 described implements found at Hoxne, Suffolk, as belonging 'to a very remote period indeed even beyond that of the modern world'. In the middle of the last century the great age of these humanly manufactured flint tools was officially recognized by the geological world as a result of reports published by Hugh Falconer, Sir Joseph Prestwich and (Sir) John Evans. The Frenchman Boucher de Perthes collected and studied these Palaeolithic (Old Stone Age) tools in the Somme valley in Northern France, and in the early years of this century V. Commont inaugurated systematic research in the same area by studying the sequence of river gravels and silts in which stone implements were found imbedded. The expansion of these studies went hand in hand with the development of the geology and palaeontology of the Pleistocene period. When the evolutionary view of biology was established, interest arose in interpreting flint implements as documents of human evolution and in relation to the skeletal remains of prehistoric man. A satisfactory correlation between stone cultures and the various types of fossil man has not been achieved, but enough is known to give a general picture and to encourage the belief that future discoveries will add to it.

TIME

A discussion of the stone tools and stone-working techniques in which the earliest story of mankind is recorded must begin by putting the subject in its proper time-perspective. All the most ancient relics of man so far discovered, both human skeletal fragments and humanly fashioned stones, belong to the Pleistocene[1] period of geology and so fall within the last two million years of the Earth's history. The beginning of this period is ill defined,[2] but its main course was punctuated in certain areas by large-scale glaciations. Surviving traces of the passage of the ice are easily recognized, and provide the basis of a chronological scheme, enabling us to determine within broad limits the order and date of some important developments in the early evolution of man and his culture.

In the preceding Tertiary era (a large geological division embracing perhaps seventy million years) the climate of Europe had varied from warm to sub-tropical. But soon after the beginning of the Pleistocene, geographical changes, probably aided by slight variations in the reception of the sun's radiation at the Earth's surface, led to a change of seasonal temperatures. It is argued that in the polar regions and at high altitudes slightly warmer winters produced a greater snowfall, while decreased summer temperatures caused less melting and allowed the ice to accumulate from year to year. Whatever the precise climatic causes, it is certain

[1] The latest major division of geological time is the Quaternary. It has two subdivisions: the Pleistocene, beginning nearly two million years ago and ending about 10,000 years ago; and the succeeding Flandrián or postglacial period, which continues to the present.
[2] The definition now most widely adopted places the beginning of the period at the point in time when true horse, elephant and ox appeared and spread widely. This seems to have been earlier than the onset of the first recognized glaciation.

that the polar ice-caps increased their area in at least some directions, and that from the more elevated mountain regions ice grew outwards in the form of valley glaciers or as extensive sheets, hundreds of feet thick, on flatter ground. The Alps and the Himalayas, the Laurentians and the Rocky Mountains, the highlands of Scandinavia and Britain became centres of ice formation. To the glaciation of Britain ice was contributed from her own mountains and from Scandinavia.

There is ample evidence to show that glaciation did not occur as a single event. The ice fronts fluctuated frequently, these fluctuations being subordinated to at least three great advances and retreats preceded by one or two earlier and less important episodes.[1] The advances are known as Glaciations and the intervening periods as Interglacials. The terminology adopted by British geologists for these periods is to call the glaciations after the major ice-sheets recognised in North Germany, which are known respectively as (1) the Elster (2) the Saale and (3) the Weichsel. The interglacials are (1) the Cromerian (2) the Hoxnian and (3) the Eemian. Of these the first two (the Cromerian which precedes the Elster Glaciation and the Hoxnian which precedes the Saale Glaciation) are named after internationally famous British interglacial lake deposits. Between a major retreat and the following major advance the climate of Europe could be much as it is today, even warmer, and the ice shrank to something like its present distribution. At its greatest extension the ice covered Europe with an unbroken mantle southwards to a line running approximately east-west through Central Germany and along the northern edge of the Thames valley. A little further south the Alpine ice grew and shrank similarly. During a glacial maximum the northern part of the Asiatic and American continents and the mountainous backbone of Europe and Asia must have resembled present-day Greenland.

[1] The 'retreat' of a glacier does not of course imply a reversed, backward movement of the ice itself. The iceflow continued in the same direction as hitherto, but since melting now exceeded the supply of fresh ice, the *front* of the glacier withdrew over the ground of its previous advance.

The evidence for the coming and going of the ice is provided by geology. Being fed at their centre the ice-sheets and glaciers were in constant movement. Besides producing grandiose effects on the landscape by scooping out and rounding the bottoms of valleys, they left traces of their passage in the form of characteristic clays and gravels constituted by materials collected and transported by the ice. These glacial deposits are found today distributed in patterns reflecting the ice movement and melting. The rock debris incorporated in the bottom layers of the moving ice formed boulder-clay or till, a more or less clayey deposit irregularly mixed with stones of all sizes. The melting of the ice along the edge of the ice-field tended to slow down the advance of the ice-front. When the supply of ice was equal to the amount lost by melting the ice-front became stable, and along it gravel, boulder-clay and rock-fragments transported by the ice were formed into great banks—the terminal moraines—which today still constitute impressive topographical features. In advance of the terminal moraines ridges and fans of gravel, sand and rock-flour were spread by streams of water issuing from the ice during summer melting. Frequently such deposits of glacial origin are found above or below or interspersed with water-laid deposits which are shown by their contained animal and plant remains to have been formed in periods of warmer climate. This direct evidence of the alternation of glacial and warmer 'interglacial' phases is one of the principal means of constructing the geological calendar of the Pleistocene.

Another important means of building the Pleistocene chronology and extending its application beyond the glaciated area is provided by the terraces found on the sides of river-valleys. These terraces record past variations in the river's down-cutting power, and their formation is very complex. Two principles, however, stand out: the river tends to erode its bed downwards when its water supply is increased or when its level relative to the sea rises. The supply of water, being dependent on climate, must have corresponded in some way with the advance and retreat of the ice. But it is the change of level which has proved most useful for chronology, and the theory of this process is here outlined first. A relative rise in level of a river bed above the sea may result from an uplift of the land. In some parts of the world, particularly in Central and East Africa, this factor has considerably influenced terrace formation, and its effects cannot so far be related to the glacial chronology. But in Europe and in other regions where the land mass is more stable, it was chiefly the periodic fall of the sea which gave rivers their relative elevation and their consequently increased eroding power. These Pleistocene fluctuations in sea-level were linked directly to the waxing and waning of the ice-sheets, obeying a similar rhythm: during a glacial phase so much water was absorbed from the sea into the ice-sheets covering the land that the sea-level fell some scores or even hundreds of feet. When the warmer climate of an interglacial phase caused melting, the sea-level rose again. The behaviour of rivers conformed to these fluctuations. During a glacial low sea-level, their channels were deepened, the erosion proceeding upstream from the mouth; given time the deepening might work back to the upper course. The rising sea-level of the succeeding interglacial phase caused rivers to fill their channels in the lower part of their course with gravels and silts; but this process of filling, or aggradation, was confined to the lower course. As the sea-level again fell in the next glacial phase, and rivers again eroded their beds downwards, fragments of the gravel filling remained clinging to the valley sides in the form of a terrace, sometimes continuous over a long distance, but often broken up and difficult to distinguish by eye.

Valleys frequently have several such terraces, spaced at varying heights above the present floor, so that the valley sides are shaped into a number of gigantic steps. It follows from the mechanism of their formation that the terraces preserved on valley sides were formed at successively later dates, the highest being the oldest: for a river-bed formed at a higher level would destroy or bury an earlier terrace formed at a lower level. This gradation of levels is particularly well developed in the lower and tidal reaches of rivers, where the terrace levels must correspond more or less closely to the heights at which the sea-level became stabilized at successive periods. Geologists have not yet found a final answer to the question: why should the sea not have risen to approximately the same height during each interglacial? A possible explanation is that throughout Late Tertiary and Pleistocene times the level of sea, in addition to its ice-controlled fluctuations, was continually dropping. The importance of the terrace gradation for archaeology is that the sequence of terraces can be brought into relation with the sequence of glacial deposits previously described, and so becomes one of the principal means of discovering the time order of Pleistocene events.

In the middle and lower part of its course, the Thames valley has three main steps, at heights of approximately 100, 50 and 25 feet above the present river, the first two corresponding respectively to the last but one interglacial and the last interglacial. The 25-foot terrace is generally held to correlate with a high sea-level also of the last interglacial, later than that represented by the 50-foot terrace.

In the upper portion of river valleys the effects of rising and falling sea-level are absent or much reduced, and a variety of local factors, such as river-capture and the outcrop of hard rocks, complicates the mechanics of terrace-formation. In some instances it is clear that the deposits composing an upstream terrace, in contrast to the interglacial deposition on the lower course, were laid down in a cold climatic phase. Thus the lower part of the Summertown terrace of the Thames in Oxfordshire contains the bones of cold-climate animals. A possible explanation of this reversal of the process deduced from the lower-course terraces involves the second major factor in terrace-formation, namely the variation of water-supply. As a cold phase developed, the severe winter freezing robbed the river of its customary supply of water, and melting during progressively cooler summers did not compensate the loss. At the same time the amount of solid material which reached the river in the form of rock debris and soil was greatly increased; for frost broke up the rock, and the vegetation which serves to secure the soil in warmer conditions had been destroyed by the cold. The river received a greater load of solid material at a time when its power of transportation was reduced. The load was consequently deposited in the river channel, which was gradually filled. When with the return of warm climate the river revived enough to resume erosion in the normal way, the edges of the cold-climate bed were left behind as terraces.

Owing to the geological complexities in the formation of upstream terraces, the significance of their relative heights above the modern stream in connexion with the alternation of glacial and interglacial climate, and with variations of sea-level is, generally speaking, less well established than in the case of the terraces of the lower course; and the upstream terraces have so far furnished less dating evidence. In the middle part of the Thames the two terrace régimes may overlap, and chronological deduction is accordingly more intricate.

Another type of deposit which is important in interpreting Pleistocene geology results from solifluxion (i.e. 'soil-flow'), a process which may be observed in the vicinity of modern ice-sheets. When the summer warmth causes the ice to melt but is insufficient to unfreeze the subsoil, the undrained melt-water reduces the top-soil to a mobile sludge. Observation has shown that a slope of as little as one degree is enough to set this sludge in motion. Deposits formed in this manner on valley sides have a very varied appearance; they usually show signs of crumpling and compression, and have none of the regularities of fluviatile deposition, the constituent fragments being unstratified and frequently unworn. Where such deposits are thick and widespread they may indicate a phase of cold climate, corresponding in some cases to one of the extensions of the Pleistocene ice as established on other evidence. Solifluxion deposits are variously known in England as trail, head and coombe rock. The Main Coombe Rock is an important cold-climate formation in the lower Thames valley.

East Anglia provides the bulk of the evidence for the British sequence. The evidence for the first period of arctic climate in Britain appears to be in the cooling of the sea around our south-eastern coast, reflected in the sudden increase in the proportion of arctic shells found in the Newer Red Crag and the Weybourne Crag. In the later glacial phases the ice spread to southern Britain, but while it appears that three separate glaciations are to be reckoned with, not more than two boulder-clays have been found superimposed, so that the evidence of the direct kind is lacking. The major ice advances in East Anglia, represented by sheets of boulder-clay or till are known as the Lowestoft Till, the Gipping Till and the Hunstanton Till. The correlation between East Anglia and the Thames presents many problems. An example of a crucial debated point is the Main Coombe Rock of the lower Thames valley referred to above. This is a deposit formed under arctic conditions, presumably on the fringe of the ice-field itself, but it is at present uncertain whether the Coombe Rock corresponds to parts of the Gipping Till or the Hunstanton Till. The evidence for interglacials is of two types. The post-crag interglacial is best represented by the remains of warmth-loving flora and fauna in the Cromer Forest Bed. The next interglacial is now generally accepted as represented in East Anglia by the lake deposits at Hoxne interstratified between two boulder clays. As already outlined above, interglacial deposits are also represented in the aggradation terraces of the river Thames.

In the northern hemisphere between the fronts of the northern ice and the ice of the more southerly mountain ranges stretched a zone of tundra country, resembling the northern region of Asia as it is today, sparsely inhabited by arctic animals, with thin and stunted vegetation. Over the tundra zone blew powerful winds which eroded the ungrassed soil from some areas and re-deposited it in others as a thick blanket of dust. Today the loess, as this wind-borne deposit is called, constitutes an extremely fine-grained, structureless soil,[1] widespread in south-eastern Europe, South Russia (the Steppes) and Central China. In places it is divisible into horizontal zones answering to glacial phases and thus makes a further contribution to chronology.

The problem of dating the appearances of prehistoric man in the Pleistocene period generally resolves itself into the task of relating his stone tools and his bones to the succession of geological events above described. This means in almost every case that the tools and bones must be found buried and undisturbed, *in situ*, in geological deposits referable to the established succession. The men of the earlier Pleistocene often lived on the banks of lakes and rivers, so that their stone tools are found favourably situated for geological dating, in fluviatile gravels and ancient lake beds. Research in the valleys of the Thames and the Somme first supplied a provisional chronological sequence of stone tool-types, which, grouped in cultures according to their shapes and techniques of production, formed the basis of a general classification.

During the severe cold phases of the last glaciation, European tribes took shelter in caves and at the foot of the cliffs, instead of migrating southwards, as some of their predecessors seem to have done. The massive deposits at such sites, occupation debris rich in cultural remains, are difficult to link with the glacial scheme, so that their position within the last glaciation may be uncertain. The age of the cave-cultures of Europe relative to each other is established in fair detail by the study of their successive appearances in distinct strata in the filling of many caves.

On the evidence so far discussed the dating of cultures can only be relative to each other and not absolute in terms of years. From the evolutionary point of view, it is the succession of events which has primary importance, and it is just such evidence of sequence which the geologist is best able to supply. It is thus not surprising that widely divergent speculative answers were for long given to the obscurer question of absolute age.

[1] The fertility of the loess is as much appreciated today as it was by the pioneering Neolithic farmers, who sought it out for settlement.

More certain evidence is offered by the study of radio-active substances. The atoms of these are unstable and tend to break down into atoms of other elements giving off 'radiations' in the process. The rates at which these processes occur follow known laws and are unaffected by external influences, so that a measurement of time can be based upon them. By these means interesting results have been reached in calculating the ages of the earlier divisions of geological time. In applying them to the Pleistocene period two lines of investigations have been followed. One relies on radio-active substances present in sea-water and incorporated in deep-sea sediments. Specimens of sediment from the bed of the north Atlantic have been collected and their ages calculated. The correlation of the dates so obtained with phases of glaciation depends on the presence in the sediment of foraminifera and other organic matter which suggest a definite climatic environment.

A more direct method is that which uses radio-active carbon. Carbon 14 is a radio-active isotope of ordinary carbon formed from atmospheric nitrogen as a result of the action of cosmic rays. It suffers radio-active decay, reverting slowly to nitrogen. Being present in the atmosphere together with ordinary carbon (both in the form of carbon dioxide) it is incorporated in the tissue of all living things through their vital processes. When an organism dies it can no longer replenish its carbon 14 atoms. As it continues to break down, the carbon 14 previously absorbed is reduced in quantity, the reduction proceeding at a predictable rate. It is thus possible to calculate the age of dead organic material from a measurement of its residual carbon 14.

This method of time measurement has not yet been widely applied in Europe, but it promises much. Two dates are particularly interesting here: the age of charcoal found in the floor deposit of the Lascaux cave (p. 66 note), is estimated as 15,516, plus or minus 900, from the present; and a Magdalenian level at La Garenne, also in the Dordogne, as 12,986, plus or minus 560, from the present. Radiocarbon dating is confined to the last glaciation and the post-glacial period as dates rarely exceed 70,000 B.C. The method cannot unfortunately be extended far enough into the past to embrace the earliest cultures and the first traces of human life.

Estimates of the absolute age of such early cultures have been obtained from radioactivity measurements of volcanic deposits contemporary with the early remains. These measurements depend on the radioactive decay of potassium 40 to the inert gas argon. Most igneous rocks contain potassic minerals, and with the decay of potassium 40, the gas argon slowly accumulates in the rock at a predictable rate. From measurements of the relative amounts of potassium and argon in a rock, it is therefore possible to estimate its date of formation. The method has been used successfully to date rocks of earlier periods, but its extension into the field of Pleistocene dating raises technical problems of measuring extremely small quantities of argon. Since, in some rocks, argon can be lost through diffusion, the method cannot be applied with equal success to all volcanic rocks. However, some interesting results have been obtained for the fossil hominid *H. erectus* of Java, which is dated to $\frac{1}{2}$ million years, and results for the pebble cultures at Olduvai range from 1 million years to $1\frac{3}{4}$ million years.

The most striking recent discoveries of human bones and stone cultures have been in Java, China, and particularly Africa. Accordingly a beginning has been made with the task of extending the Pleistocene time-scale beyond the confines of the glaciated area and its immediate periphery. The most promising link is provided by the fluctuations of sea-level, since these must have been distributed throughout the intercommunicating seas of the world. Ancient beaches and marine erosion features raised above the modern sea on the North African coast provide a sequence of high-level pauses of the sea which broadly correlates with the deductions made from the terrace history of the Thames and the Somme; but the details of this correlation require elaboration, and the evidence for extending it inland in Africa and applying its principles in other distant regions is still to be sought. Research on the deposits of the Nile valley has, however, brought Egypt into the orbit of the chronology.

Apart from intrinsic evidence of glacial origin or direct connexion with glacial phenomena, the only means of assigning the formation of a deposit to a cold or a warm climatic phase is the study of the fossils (principally bones, teeth and shells) it contains. Some mollusca and mammals are sensitive indicators in this respect; others, more catholic in their choice of environment, are less useful. Moreover, some fast-evolving mammals permit a limited measure of chronological comparison. Thus *Elephas meridionalis*, which became extinct in Europe in the Elster glaciation, may in that region serve to identify deposits of the Cromerian interglacial. The straight-tusked species, *Elephas antiquus*, adapted to a warm or temperate woodland habitat, appears in Europe in the interglacials and dies out before the last (Eemian) glaciation. Finally, the mammoth, *Elephas primigenius*, specialized for life in sub-arctic conditions and on tundra vegetation, is particularly characteristic of the last glaciation, when it was the prey of the Upper Palaeolithic hunters. Woolly rhinoceros and reindeer also betoken cold climate, the latter being typical of last glaciation times in Europe. The hippopotamus and Merck's rhinoceros reflect a warm wooded environment. The cave lion and the hyena, on the other hand, show no marked preference in their choice of habitat, being found wherever their prey existed. The faunal grouping and sequence naturally vary from region to region according to local climatic and geographical conditions, and chronological deductions from them are frequently insecure. In Africa, where faunal dating evidence would be particularly valuable, it is found that only in early Pleistocene deposits is the fossil fauna significantly different from the modern animal population.

About 20,000 years ago the last Pleistocene ice-sheets began to withdraw from North Germany. The end of the Pleistocene period and the beginning of the Recent or Holocene is conventionally fixed at the withdrawal of the ice from a belt of moraines formed during a pause in South Sweden and Finland. This final withdrawal began about 8000 B.C. During the period of these glacial retreats a new method of dating is available. A Swede, Baron de Geer, made use of the fact that deposits formed on the beds of melt-water lakes situated along the ice-front during the final retreat have a horizontally banded structure. According to de Geer, each pair of bands represents one year's deposition, the thicker of the two being the result of heavier deposition during summer melting. By counting these layers in the path of the glacial retreat, linking one ancient lake-bed to another through exact tallies of sections of layer-series, de Geer calculated that the ice-sheets had left Denmark and paused in South Sweden by 13,200 B.C. and that in 6839 B.C. the ice-cap covering the Scandinavian highlands had shrunk to the point of splitting in two at its centre.

Another geological feature of the Scandinavian area which has been exploited for its chronological implications is a series of shore lines, now raised above sea-level, which were formed in the last stage of the melting of the ice, and at various times in the Recent period. Two independent vertical movements are recorded: the rise of the sea which accompanied the final melting, and the belated recovery of the Scandinavian land-mass from the depression it had suffered under the weight of the ice. By correlating de Geer's dates and the raised shorelines archaeologists have been able to use his theory to date many sites found near the coast. Whether or not de Geer's exact year count be accepted the *relative* dates derived from the post-glacial variations of sea-level must be valid. Beyond the area of the Scandinavian land recovery there was a compensatory movement which lowered the level of Northern Germany and the southern part of England and allowed the sea to gain on the land.

Botanical research has yielded results which provide another means of approximate dating and illuminate the environment of human life in the remote past. The pollen of many trees and plants is found preserved in peat and silt, and the variation of species and the proportion of species from bottom to top of these deposits illustrates the history of plant life in a non-glacial period. The post glacial sequence has been studied in some detail. (See chronological table III.) The appearance of arctic plants marks the first revival of vegetation after the departure of the ice. Birch and pine replace this tundra. Next, in a period of more continental climate (i.e. with warm summers and cooler winters) hazel joins the pine, and birch decreases. This is followed by the dominance of a mixed forest of oak, alder and lime during a period of moister climate extending down to Neolithic times, when the interference of man in many areas affected the composition of the forest.

In the post-glacial period, however, geological dating is seldom available. The remains of Mesolithic, Neolithic and later cultures are generally found on the ground surface or covered by little more than the top-soil, and the time sequence is for the most part established without recourse to geology, by noting the stratification of one culture over another at sites which were settled at different periods; and by the comparative study of characteristic forms of pottery, tools, weapons and ornaments. This comparison of types, or *typology*, represents a new chronological principle: the variations (development or degeneration) of artifacts are taken as an indication of the passage of time and hence of relative age. The manifest pitfalls of the method (chance resemblance, survival of older types alongside newer, bad workmanship simulating primitiveness, doubt whether the direction of change is progress or degeneration) make it unreliable when applied to the isolated stone implements surviving from the earlier and from many of the later Stone Age cultures. On the other hand, when cultural advance has produced a varied and distinctive equipment, and a characteristic selection of objects from this equipment has survived for comparison, the typological method is a valuable means of classifying and dating cultures. It finds its earliest satisfactory application in the cultures of the last glacial period (the 'Upper Palaeolithic'). To establish date, typology must be supported by other chronological evidence, and it is important, as has been done in the foregoing account, to keep such evidence apart from the indications implicit in types. Typological schemes have, in fact, their greatest value when they can be tied to a chronology dependent on external records, as happens when commercial links can be traced between prehistoric Europe and the literate and calendar-minded civilizations of the Near East.

THE RAW MATERIAL

When man took to fashioning stone tools he soon discovered that tough, fine-grained rocks were the most suitable material. They are capable of forming strong cutting-edges and points, and since they break with a more or less regular and dependable fracture they lend themselves to purposive shaping better than do softer and coarser rocks. Flint and its near relative, chert, one or both of which are easily available over large areas of the world, possess the requisite qualities of hardness and evenness to a high degree. When flint and chert were lacking or present only in unsuitably small pieces prehistoric man used the next best material, usually a quartzitic or basaltic rock. Diorite, chalcedony, jadeite, granite, etc., were used at one time or another, but never, it seems, in preference to fresh flint if this was to be had. In Burma fossilized wood proved to be the best local material, and its fibrous structure influenced to some extent the forms of tools. Indurated shale was popular in the Old Stone Age of South Africa. In Kenya in late Stone Age times and in Melos and other parts of the Aegean in the Neolithic and Bronze Ages much use was made of the natural black volcanic glass called obsidian. When compelled to do so, prehistoric communities were capable of organizing trade in tool material over surprisingly long distances; but the evidence for such trade—as also for the deliberate mining of flint from the Chalk—is confined to later times. Neolithic peoples traded the honey-coloured flint of Le Grand Pressigny in Central France, Graig Lwyd rock from Penmaenmawr in North Wales and the greenstones of Brittany and Cornwall. In Norfolk and Sussex neolithic miners extracted fresh flint nodules from mines dug deep in the Chalk.

It must not be thought that in the Stone Age stone was the only material used for tools and weapons. From the Upper (i.e. later) Palaeolithic onwards the archaeological record shows that antler and bone were fashioned into harpoons, needles, borers and picks, all implements fundamental to the primitive economy. Although stone artifacts are almost the sole survivals from the cultural equipment of the earlier Stone Age tribes, there is no reason to suppose that other, perishable, materials were not used. We may assume that prehistoric man in addition to stone worked at least wood, from which very satisfactory fire-hardened points and cutting-edges can be made. Modern primitive peoples make casual use of a great variety of materials, ranging from shell and sharks' teeth to the bottle-glass and telegraph insulators of their civilized neighbours.

It is convenient to describe the physical properties of the tool material separately before entering on the various techniques of working it which prevailed at different times in the prehistoric period. Flint, the favourite material, is here described in detail. The fracture of other kinds of stone resembles that of flint in so far as they approach it in hardness, fineness and evenness of texture. Another physical feature of special interest to the archaeologist is the condition of the stone surface. Long exposure alters the surface of all kinds of stone. Flint and chert[1] are peculiarly susceptible to the effects of weathering, and their altered surface readily assumes mineral colouring (patination) from contact with gravel and soil.

[1] The term 'chert' is usually reserved for the less pure siliceous concretions formed in calcareous formations other than chalk, but its application is not very clearly defined. The term 'flint' is used in the following section of this manual to denote not only that derived from the chalk, but other material of like texture.

FLINT

Petrologists define flint as a 'mosaic-like structure of colloidal silica (opal) and crypto-crystalline silica (the form of quartz known as chalcedony) in variable proportions.' It occurs in limestone, especially in the European Chalk, in the form of nodules of irregular and often fantastic shape, sometimes up to eighteen inches in length, laid in horizontal or vertical strings, or sometimes as continuous horizontal sheets—called tabular flint—up to three inches in thickness. The silica of which the flint is composed was derived from the glass-like skeletons of sponges inhabiting the seas in which the Chalk and other limestone deposits were laid down. As these deposits were being uplifted and hardening into rock, water charged with some solvent of silica, probably atmospheric carbonic acid, dissolved the sponge remains. Under altered conditions of pressure this silica was precipitated from solution at distinct levels in the rock, replacing the limestone and solidifying as nodular or continuous tabular concretions. Frequently the silica grew round a mineral fragment or marine fossil as nucleus; hence the curious structures which may be revealed when a nodule is broken across. But however suggestive they are to the imaginative, the outer shape and inner structure of these nodules formed between 100 and 70 million years ago have no archaeological significance.

Wherever the Chalk or other limestone matrix has weathered away, the flint, which is more resistant, is left exposed on the ground, often to be included later in river gravels and other superficial deposits. In English Chalk country flints are the commonest surface stones. Even when the chalk has disappeared entirely the flints often remain. The outer surface of both nodular and tabular flint, when it is freshly extracted from the mother rock, is covered with a tough, rough, whitish skin, called the *cortex*. Fresh breaks show that the flint itself is usually black, though it may vary from dark blue to brown, yellow, red or white. It may even be banded with different colours.

Seen in a fragment of any thickness it is opaque. Newly fractured, this internal flint yields a smooth lustrous surface, which, after very long exposure to the weather and to chemical salts in the soil, changes colour. The skin of altered colour so formed, the *patina*, is quite distinct from the native colouring of the body of the flint. Certain native colours may characterize the flint of particular geographical areas, making it possible sometimes to trace to their regional source pieces of flint transported by glacial action or the hand of man. Lincolnshire, for example, has a characteristic grey flint, while in East Anglia and Kent the flint is typically black. In the ancient gravels of the Thames valley at Swanscombe, Kent, occurs a brown and yellow banded variety of flint derived from the dark green-skinned nodules of the 'bull-head' bed which underlies the Thanet Sand. In all kinds of flint the uniform grain may be interrupted by knots of greater toughness and sometimes of different colour. These reveal themselves in the fracture, the evenness of which they often destroy.

It is important to distinguish the different types of fracture to which flint is prone. We begin with *mechanical fracture*, which results from a blow struck in a determinate direction and delivered on a relatively small area—the 'point of impact'.

Fig. 1 *a* to *d* shows a piece of tabular flint, drawn in section, being subjected to increasingly powerful blows at point X. At position *a* a light blow has produced a crack which penetrates only a small distance into the body of the material. The shape of the fracture is conical, the apex of the cone being at the point of impact. Seen from above the fracture appears as a small circle, probably surrounded by a patch of discoloration due to the interference of the crack with the passage of light through the flint. The stronger the blow the further the conical fracture penetrates, until finally it reaches the other side of the tablet and the detached cone of flint falls away, as shown at position *d* of fig. 1. In practice such an ideal fracture is very difficult to achieve because other shattering effects of the blows tend to destroy the evenness of the cone or to break the lump of flint into irregular

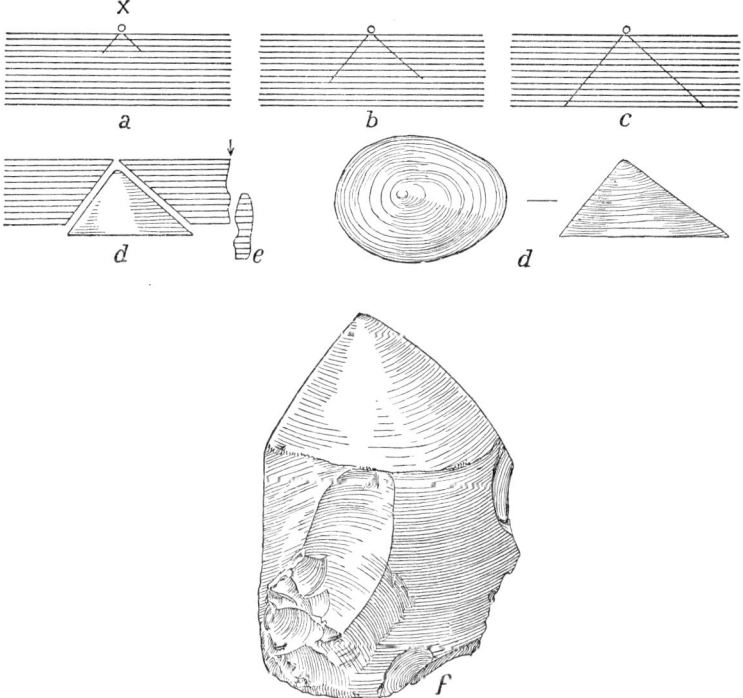

FIG. 1. Cones of percussion. (*Scale* 2/3.)
(*a—d*) Theoretical stages in the fracture. (*e*) A flake removed with incomplete conical fracture. (*f*) An actual cone preserved intact (i.e. corresponding to *d*).

pieces. In nature the production of a perfect cone is hardly to be expected at all. The normal case of mechanical fracture, both in working flint and in natural breakage, is the detachment of a flake from the side of a piece of flint, as shown in fig. 1 *e*. In shaping flint a projecting angle of the block is chosen on which the flaking blow can be conveniently delivered. This edge is known as the *striking platform*. One side of the detached flake, its back, is part of the original surface of the parent block. The other face is formed by the fracture and is called the *main flake surface.* This main flake surface shows a swelling or *bulb* arising from a point just below the striking platform, and probably other features are noticeable, such as ripples and straight lines. This type of fracture is known as 'conchoidal' (i.e.

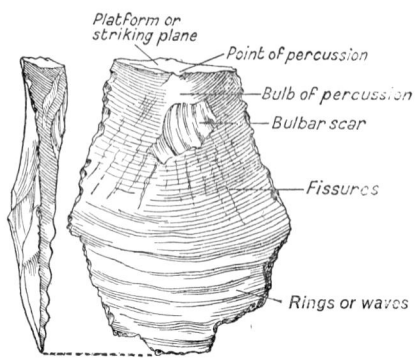

FIG. 2. The ideal flake, in which all the conchoidal features are clearly visible. (*Scale* 2/3.)

'mussel-shell'), and the full list of its characteristics is as follows (fig. 2):

A positive (convex) bulb of percussion, frequently developing into a conical segment near the point of impact.

A negative (concave) scar of irregular shape on this bulb, marking the place from which a small chip of flint springs away on fracture (éraillure).

Irregular straight fissures visible below the bulb and radiating from the point of impact.

A number of concentric ripples with their common centre at the point of impact.

Frequently only two or three of the conchoidal features can be recognized, the bulb nearly always being one of these. The development of the other features varies with the direction of the flaking blow, and also with the hardness of the material used to strike the blow. For blows of constant force, flakes struck off with a stone or metal hammer have more prominent and concentrated bulbs than flakes struck with a striker of bone or wood. On the whole the more resilient the striker, the flatter and more diffused the bulbs and ripples, until they become almost invisible to the eye. The bulb is a distorted segment of the complete cone illustrated in fig. 1 d. On the parent block the scar left by the removal

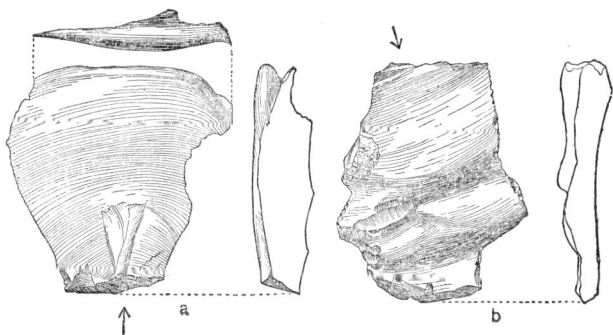

FIG. 3. (a) Flake terminating in a hinge fracture. (b) Flake with exaggerated ripples. The arrows show the direction of striking. (Scale 1/3.)

of the flake has the conchoidal features in reverse, a hollow called the negative bulb of percussion taking the place of the positive bulb of the flake.

Sometimes the plane of the fracture, instead of approaching the surface of the block at a steady angle, tapering out and so leaving a sharp edge on the end of the flake, turns abruptly outwards and leaves the edge of the flake blunt and smoothly rounded. This *hinge-fracture*, as it is called (fig 3), may be caused by one of the conchoidal ripples, or it may happen that the angle of the flaking blow directs the fracture too steeply into the body of the flint, so that the fracturing force, instead of expending itself inside the flint without completing the break, takes a short cut to the outside. Hinge-fractures are particularly liable to be mistaken for polishing, the handiwork of man. The behaviour of the fracture is also affected by the relation of the flint block to its surroundings at the moment of impact, whether it is lying on or imbedded in hard or soft material, whether it is touching this material over a great or small proportion of its surface; if it be held in the hand, whether the point of support is nearer or further removed from the striking platform. In unfavourable circumstances the waves of stress set up in the flint when it is struck may avoid resolution as a clean conchoidal fracture and exert instead a shattering force which breaks the flint at unexpected places and perhaps into many pieces. Theoretical explanations of these reactions to percussion are obscure and afford no practical help in working flint. A little time spent in experiment on a nodule of flint with a variety of strikers will teach more than the most detailed description.

Flint can also be broken by blows without human intervention. Flakes are struck off against boulders in the tumbling waters of a stream, or by a rock falling from a height, and may have the marks of conchoidal fracture. We should be wrong therefore in taking the mere presence of a bulb of percussion as proof that the flake was struck by the hand of man. Experience will to some extent teach the difference between flakes produced by man and the fortuitous flakes of nature. One may begin by noting the difference between the bulbs of percussion on the fragments of a flint gravel produced as road-metal in a crushing machine (in conditions approximating to the casualness of nature), with the bulbs of an indisputable human flake or blade industry, such as is found in the Palaeolithic or the Neolithic periods. The bulbs of the artifact flakes are better defined, but *there is no purely technical criterion for distinguishing human work from natural chance.* It is true nevertheless that the greater part of the breakage suffered by flint in nature is not caused by mechanical blows, but by change of temperature. *Thermal fracture can* however be recognized and discarded as of non-human origin. In cold weather either the contraction of the material itself or the expansion of freezing water in pockets and cracks exerts sufficient force to break the nodule. Thermal breaks may at first sight be confused with mechanical breaks, but attention to what was said above about mechanical fracture will show the difference. Apart from occasional shallow rings, thermal fracture does not display conchoidal characteristics, the fracture surface is duller and less smooth than that resulting from a mechanical blow. Certain freaks of thermal breakage should be carefully noted, for they are

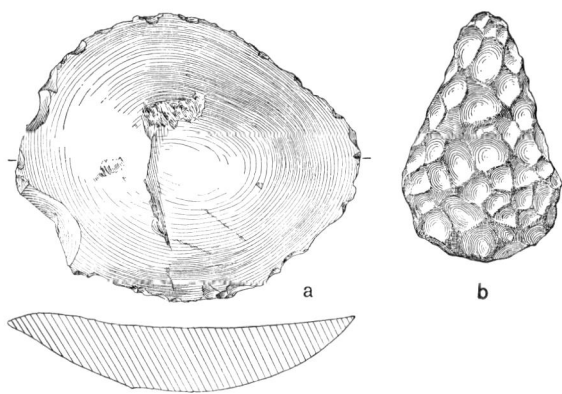

FIG. 4. (*a*) 'Pot-lid' fracture. (*b*) Frost-pitting. (*Scale* 2/5.)

traps for the unwary. A *pot-lid* fracture (fig. 4) may have shallow ripples, but the centre around which these ripples are arranged lies approximately in the middle of the fracture surface, and hence not at a point of impact as in a mechanical fracture. Moreover, thermal fracture is not accompanied by a bulbar scar or fissures. The scar left by the thermal flake, unless it be interfered with by knots in the texture of the flint, is a shallow, more or less symmetrical hollow, and the comparatively dull surface has a *pulled away* appearance in comparison with the *struck off* appearance of mechanical fracture. Fig. 4 shows another peculiar thermal effect known as *frost-pitting* in which the flint surface is covered with small contiguous hollows resembling little pot-lid craters, but less regular. This condition is sometimes mistaken for human chipping. Even more surprising is the columnar fracture (fig. 5) called *starch-fracture*. Here the lustreless facets of the column have none of the conchoidal characteristics. Of all the thermal forms this most often receives undeserved honours as a human product.

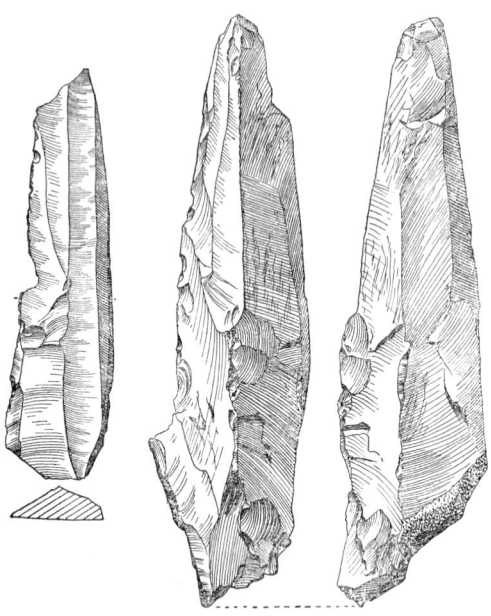

FIG. 5. 'Starch' (i.e. columnar) fracture. (*Scale* 2/5.)

When it is deprived of its protective cortex and exposed on open ground directly to atmospheric effects, or, if underground, to the effects of percolating rain-water, flint suffers a chemical alteration of its surface which results in a change of colour. This process is known as patination, and the colour it imparts to the surface must be distinguished from the original body-colour discussed above. The acid in rain-water dissolves from the surface of the flint its more soluble constituent, the opaline silica. This leaves a porous meshwork of minute crystals which scatter the light instead of absorbing it as the unimpaired flint does, and consequently the surface assumes a white, or, in the early stage of the process, a bluish colour. This change, in which nothing is added, may continue until a considerable depth of surface is affected and the dark core of unaltered flint is buried in a thick opaque crust. Sometimes no unaltered flint remains at all. A long time is required for patination, which is therefore some evidence of antiquity. An experiment recently made showed that flint becomes patinated when it is exposed to rain-water charged with the gaseous products of decaying vegetation acting in the presence of chalk. Despite continuous submersion in an artificial medium much more concentrated than nature supplies, twenty-two months were required to produce a patina 0·01 mm. thick.

Once the surface is rendered porous, it readily absorbs mineral salts from the soil or gravel with which it comes into contact. The colours which it then assumes may be very striking: all shades of red, brown, ochre, yellow and green are found.[1] Since the colour reflects the chemical composition of the containing or underlying deposit, it often happens that particular colouring is common to the flints found in a certain area, and if sufficiently distinctive it may even serve to indicate the find-place of an implement. When flints have lain in or on chalk, their patina is usually unstained and white. This is true of the surface flints of the Cotswolds and the Sussex Downs. Near the Fens, on the other hand, the flints are frequently coloured dark brown by the peat. A speckled patina of yellow and green (known to collectors as 'toad-belly' patina) is peculiar to surface implements found on Warren Hill in Suffolk. Flints contained in gravel usually acquire some shade of yellow or brown from contact with iron salts. With the help of patination and mineral colouring it is often possible to refer a loose surface flint to a nearby geological deposit in which it originally lay; or to separate two series of flints which have different geological histories, and hence may be of different age,

---

[1] For convenience the term patination is usually used for both the deopalized surface and its subsequent staining.

but which have come to be mixed together in the same geological stratum, or have been collected carelessly.

When chips are removed from a piece of patinated flint the contrasting colour of the internal flint appears in the new scars; and when the latter in their turn become patinated a difference of colour or tone generally distinguishes them from the original surface. By noting these signs of patination 'of two ages', one can sometimes identify implements which were retrimmed and re-used long after they were abandoned by their original makers. Quite apart, however, from variegation caused by chipping at different periods, the colouring of a piece of patinated flint is seldom uniform. Often mottled surfaces composed of various colours or of different shades of the same colour are merely the result of accidental variation in the intensity of patination and staining. But when one side of an implement differs wholly from the other, this may often be taken as a sign that the implement lay for a long period on the ground surface, so that the two faces were differently weathered and stained. It is probable that microscopic algae and lichens also play a part in the development of peculiar markings, particularly of those which form tree-like patterns. The ferruginous lines and spots known as 'iron-mould' may have a similar origin. They are frequently found on white patinated flints lying on the surface of the ground, the rusty marks following the flake-ridges and spreading out from them. An old belief that the marks are the effect of contact with metallic iron, for example ploughshares or the studs on ploughmen's boots, is hardly a satisfactory explanation.

The degree of patination is habitually used to argue the absolute or comparative age of flints. But the nature and rate of formation of a patina depend on so many fortuitous circumstances that it cannot be a reliable guide for dating. In conjunction with other evidence, it can give useful indications.

In natural surroundings a lump of flint may be constantly exposed to battering by repeated small blows, none powerful enough to break it through, but some capable of producing incipient cones of percussion (fig. 1 a) which allow the processes of de-opalization and staining to penetrate a short distance below the surface. The colour may in time spread over most of the surface, giving it a mottled appearance. Incipient cones of percussion are associated with the 'toad-belly' patina referred to above. A distinctive patination may also form in scratches made on the flint under great pressure by soil movement. The patinated scratches (striations) show as lines, isolated or in a network, coloured white against a darker background. Besides patination the abrasion of flint by natural forces can greatly alter the appearance it had when the nodule was first broken. Friction in gravel, sand and water over a long period blunts and smooths the original sharp ridges of flaked flint and blurs the original outline. This *rolling* is taken as evidence that the flints have been moved by natural agency, usually water, from the place where they were first left by man in their fresh state. When a flint has sharp, unabraded flake-scars (even when these are deeply patinated), it may be assumed that it has lain more or less undisturbed, *in situ*, since deposition. When a deposit of gravel or silt contains a mixture of fresh and abraded implements the two groups are often distinguished and the latter spoken of as *derived*. It is implied that the fresh flints are *in situ*, while the worn ones, having been transported to the place from elsewhere, may be quite unrelated and possibly older.

Occasionally implements are found, of various colours, with an extremely smooth and glossy surface which cannot be accounted for by any of the phenomena discussed above. The gloss seems to be confined to pieces of great antiquity which have lain buried in a gravel or silt. One suggestion is that a skin of redeposited silica has formed on the surface of the flint, but the details of the process are not known. This gloss must not be confused with the tiny patches observed on some chipped flint sickles of Neolithic times. In this instance the cause is friction against the stalks of corn or other grasses reaped by the Neolithic farmer. The gloss imparted to flint in Neolithic times by deliberate polishing is again another matter. In regions where sandy desert exists (or has in the past existed) surface flints may be abraded and acquire a characteristic smoothness from prolonged exposure to wind-blown sand.

The earliest stone tools were flaked with stone strikers, and these 'hammer-stones' were among the earliest items of human equipment. It is not until the Middle and Upper Palaeolithic, however, that identifiable specimens are commonly found, and thereafter the use of hammer-stones can be traced as late as the Early Iron Age. Pebbles put to this use are the most readily recognized, the battering of their surface being usually confined to the ends or to the wider circumference. Most of the finer flaking of flint tools was carried out with a wooden or bone bar-hammer (wood technique). These tools do not survive. However, bone *compressors*, used for detaching minute controlled flakes by the use of pressure (pressure flaking) are found in middle and upper palaeolithic industries. These are simple pieces of bone with marks where the flints have been compressed against them.

In addition to actual stone tools various other uses were found for flint by prehistoric man. The most common type are *pot-boilers*.

By '*pot-boiler*' is meant a piece of burnt flint or stone, measuring two or three inches across, which appears to have been deliberately heated in a fire. In the case of flint the surface is whitish or grey and crackled. Early pottery was incapable of resisting direct contact with flame. One way of heating water was to drop heated stones into the containing pot. One Irish archaeologist has proved experimentally that it is possible to cook meat in this manner. At dwelling-sites large heaps of these *pot-boilers* accumulated. But there may have been other domestic routines besides pot-boiling which required heated stones—e.g. corn-drying and baking. Some spreads of burnt stones may be simply hearths. '*Pot-boilers*' are not confined to any particular culture.

They are notably abundant on the homestead sites of the Early Iron Age in England.

THE CULTURE SEQUENCE

The Stone Age comprises the whole period of human culture which preceded the knowledge of metal working. At this stage of culture, stone was not the only material used in making tools, but it was the most important. From the earliest part of the Stone Age, the lower and middle Palaeolithic, objects of more perishable materials have seldom survived and our knowledge of these cultures is based on the study of stone tools alone. The prerequisites of this study, the principles of dating and the properties of the material, have been outlined. It remains to discuss the forms of tools which characterize the various cultures. The classification of these is complicated by the fact that the technological advance of mankind has proceeded at vastly different rates in different parts of the world. Prehistoric Europeans knew only stone tools at a time when Egypt and Mesopotamia worked bronze. The natives of America and New Zealand were still in their Stone Age when white men conquered them. Until quite recent times, remote Saharan tribes made flint arrowheads, and some Australian and Oceanic natives still make and use stone tools.

The terminology of the broad classification is based on the prehistoric cultures of Western Europe. The scheme is as follows:

Palaeolithic (meaning Old Stone Age) embraces the cultures of the hunting and food-gathering tribes of the Pleistocene period. The term Palaeolithic is also applied to stone-working techniques employed in these cultures, and hence is sometimes applied in a technological sense to cultures of later date. The culture of the modern food-gathering aborigines of Australia, when it is unaffected by the white man's civilization, may be described as Palaeolithic, but clearly not with any chronological implication.

The unqualified term Palaeolithic is regularly used to denote cultures of the Pleistocene.

The terms Lower, Middle and Upper Palaeolithic (meaning, according to geological usage, the early middle and late Palaeolithic) are adopted in Europe and Asia. Lower Palaeolithic is used to describe the cultures which begin the sequence in Western Europe, the hand-axes, coarse flake tools and pebble tools (Acheulean, Clactonian); Upper Palaeolithic is regularly applied to the blade cultures (Aurignacian, Magdalenian, Gravettian, Creswellian) of the last glaciation which are abundantly represented in central and West Europe; the Middle Palaeolithic in this area denotes Mousterian fine flake cultures which intervene between the two. These terms can be used in a chronological as well as a technological sense. This is incorrect. There is too great a risk of ambiguity (for example in using 'Middle Palaeolithic' to describe the flake cultures of North Africa which are contemporary with many blade cultures in Europe). This manner of subdividing the Palaeolithic is best avoided, and a technological descriptive term (blade, faceted-butt flake, etc.) substituted. The terminology adopted by archaeologists in South Africa and India substitutes for this Early, Middle and Late Stone Ages, the Late Stone Age being contemporary with the Neolithic and the Middle representing both the European middle and upper palaeolithic.

Mesolithic. In the last century a hiatus was thought to occur between the last of the Palaeolithic cultures, ending with the final departure of the ice from Europe, and the cultures which introduced the Neolithic. It has subsequently been established that in fact several distinct cultures flourished in this interval, and they have been classed as Mesolithic because they are 'meso', i.e. in the middle between the New and Old Stone Ages, now called the neolithic and the palaeolithic. The forms in which Neolithic culture subsequently appears in Central and Northern Europe frequently embody survivals from the cultures of the Mesolithic food-gatherers, whose descendants adopted and influenced the new economy. In current usage the term Mesolithic is not quite straight forward, for again it happens that in Europe the chronological division corresponding to the Mesolithic coincides with a change in the technique of stone-working so that the term Mesolithic is liable to be used by some authors in a technological sense (referring to small-blade industries with microliths) when no chronological correspondence with the European sequence is or can be implied. In connexion with the later pre-Neolithic cultures of North Africa the term is particularly inappropriate, since the main problem there is precisely the relationship of these cultures —whether they are parents or cousins—to the Upper Palaeolithic and Mesolithic of Europe. Though the term mesolithic means literally Middle Stone Age it should not be confused with the Middle Stone Age of African archaeologists which corresponds rather to the Upper Palaeolithic of Europe.

Neolithic (meaning New Stone Age) cultures are characterized by polished stone tools, and by the practice of agriculture and stock-raising and of the basic crafts of early civilization, pottery and weaving. The term was adopted originally to denote the new technique of polishing stone before its connexion with these other more fundamental activities was realized. The date at which farming appears in various parts of the world varies greatly, as the increasing precision of the chronology of this stage shows, and its duration compared with the earlier divisions of the Stone Age is quite short, in Britain for example only about 1500 years or so. In a limited geographical area where a basis for dating exists one may speak of a 'Neolithic Period' with definite chronological limits in mind. But whenever there is risk of ambiguity 'Neolithic' is best applied in its purely economic sense. In archaeological literature, however, the term is sometimes used of cultures later in date than the invention of agriculture, in which only a selection of Neolithic activities, possibly excluding farming, is practised. Thus a culture widespread in the Sahara is termed Neolithic on the evidence of its stone tools, although it is difficult to be sure that agriculture or stock-raising were included in it to any great extent. The Neolithic cultures of Europe are all contemporary with bronze-using civilizations of Egypt and Mesopotamia, and some of their stone implements show the influence of metal types.

The inconsistencies in the use of the terms explained above derive from the tendency once prevalent to look for a similar succession of technological stages in all parts of the world, and to assume that in the Old World at least these stages were traversed more or less simultaneously. As often happens in other branches of biological study, the facts of prehistory do not fit exactly into abstract categories.

Individual cultures are usually named after the place or region where their characteristic relics are chiefly found or were first collected. When this material serves to illustrate the economic life of the community, hints at its social organization, informs us on its dwellings, food, weapons, ornaments, art and superstitions—thereby arming the imagination and giving a basis of comparison with what we know of modern primitive peoples—these archaeological cultures come nearer to being cultures in the full sense, that is, distinct complexes of industrial, mental and religious activities. With the rich sealed cave deposits and rock paintings and engravings of the Upper Palaeolithic the archaeological record acquires a fullness from which we can build a picture of the way of life of the hunting tribes. In the Mesolithic the picture dims, for the survivals are fewer, then from the Neolithic onwards, thanks to the remains of settled agricultural and stock-raising communities, it continues to expand and sharpen. But for the immense stretch of time represented by Middle and Lower Palaeolithic stone tools we have very slender means of controlling our speculation. The cultures of the Lower and Middle Palaeolithic correspond to differences of stone-working methods and of tool forms intimately associated with these techniques, and can thus be little more than technological divisions. Two questions suggest themselves: what wider significance can be given to these divisions; and how reliably do stone tools continue to serve as distinguishing marks of cultures from the Upper Palaeolithic (or its equivalent outside Europe) onwards, when more abundant material is available to fill out the picture? In other words, what grounds are there for believing that in prehistoric times the technological level was intimately connected with the cultural level in other respects? The sequence of early stone industries clearly implies an increase of dexterity and intelligence, and therefore of the loom of intelligence, the social group. The force of this deduction is enhanced by the increasing precision of the dates, relative and absolute, which can be set to the stages traversed. A most interesting aspect is the possibility of linking this development with our knowledge of the early hominids [1]

As to the value of stone tools in classifying cultures, it is reassuring to find their significance in this respect confirmed in the Upper Palaeolithic of France, North Africa or the Middle East where the cultures can be distinguished by more abundant and more illuminating material than in Great Britain in this period. On the other hand, by Neolithic times the various forms of axes and arrowheads correspond less closely to the culture groups, which are defined by more striking traits, such as pottery forms, habitations, burial customs. Significant variations of stone tools are, of course, to be noted, and show a logical distribution on the map, but the differences they imply may not amount to cultural cleavage nor does their similarity necessarily point to cultural identity. No doubt one reason for this is that we are now able to give a fuller account of the cultures, but it is also because stone tools and weapons no longer have the same fundamental rôle in the economy. While men hunted and gathered their food, their weapons were closely adapted to these ends. But from the Neolithic onwards agriculture and domestic animals were the foundation of economy, and on the whole less effort was spent in perfecting stone implements. After the introduction of metal the forms of stone implements cease to be significant and the toolmakers' inventiveness is applied to the new material. Some

[1] Since this question is taken as the theme of "Man the Toolmaker", published by the British Museum (Natural History), it is not dwelt on here.

superior flint types produced in the late Neolithic and Early Bronze Age (see page 77) are no exception: they were made by people for whom bronze was a rare and expensive commodity. Metal-using communities rapidly lost the art of working stone.

THE EARLIEST TOOLS

We may assume that man first used unfashioned stones picked up at random or chosen for their convenient natural shapes. Later, when he began to shape stones purposefully, his early clumsy efforts would scarcely be distinguishable from naturally broken stones. In fact the first known tools which came from the Olduvai Gorge in Tanzania (East Africa) are simple *pebble-tools* made by knocking off one or two flakes from one side of a water-worn pebble.

The development from pebble tool cultures to hand-axe cultures has been demonstrated at the site of Olduvai Gorge. The gorge is a late Pleistocene feature which has cut through a series of early Pleistocene lake deposits. A local chronology has been established on the basis of four periods of lake sedimentation but this cannot be correlated with the European sequences. The lowest deposit Bed 1 contains the pebble culture known as Oldowan, and layers of volcanic tuff in this bed have been dated by Potassium Argon to more than one million years ago (see p. 19). In the earliest stages of the Oldowan culture, tools consist largely of pebbles which have been split with one or two blows directed from one side resulting in a rough cutting edge. Bifacially worked pebble tools, in which the edge is produced by removing flakes alternately from each side of the cutting edge predominate in the later stages. In these stages, more or less pointed tools were made with a pebble butt, and by rough trimming of the butt these tools develop into crude hand-axes. In Beds I, II and IV the hand-axe culture at Olduvai shows a development closely analogous to that observed in Western

Europe. A similar sequence of pebble tool and hand-axe cultures is also known from the coast line of North Africa in Morocco.

THE CLACTONIAN CULTURE

The most primitive type of flint industry found in Europe is one consisting of flakes and pebble tools, and apparently related to the Oldowan of Africa or to the chopping tool industries of India and the Far East. So far only sporadic industries of this type are known, the best known of which is the Clactonian Industry of East Anglia and the lower Thames valley, which is dated to the early part of the Hoxnian Interglacial, and possibly to the preceding Elster Glaciation. Recently another earlier industry of this type has been located at the site of Vertes Zollos in the Vertes mountains of Hungary, where it is found in association with an extremely early type of *Homo sapiens*. The Vertes Zollos finds which are dated to an Interstadial in the Elster Glaciation, by their occurrence in a river terrace of the Danube, and by their primitive mammalian fauna, consist of very small flakes, tools and chippers made on pebbles or flakes—a micro-Clactonian or a micro-chopping tool industry. The industry is believed to be more closely similar to the Far Eastern stone industries than to the Clactonian.

The Clactonian industry also consists of choppers and flakes. The choppers, which are very similar to Clactonian cores, consist of small flint pebbles or blades from which a number of Clactonian flakes have been detached, so as to form a rough cutting edge on one side.

Clactonian flakes are thick and squat, of varying size up to six inches across. Hand-axes are entirely absent from the culture. The cores (fig. 6) are roughly biconical, with deep biting scars indicative of a stone-on-stone working technique, and show no signs of the preliminary treatment which characterizes the Levalloisian technique. The majority of the flakes have an angle ex-

Fig. 6. Clactonian core and flake from Swanscombe, Kent. The angle indicated is characteristically obtuse. (*Scale* 1/3.)

ceeding 90 degrees between the plane of the striking platform and the plane of the main flake surface. In the basal gravels of the 100 ft. aggradation of the lower Thames are found Clactonian flakes with a distinctive dark brown glossy surface. These are regarded as the earliest Clactonian stage, being thought to derive from the previous interglacial, a date which would agree with the views of some Continental authorities on the position of the industry in the French sequence. In the same Thames gravels unabraded Clactonian implements, smaller and rather more trimmed than the earlier ones, represent the middle stage of the culture, and compare closely with the implements from the name-site, an old channel of the Thames at Clacton-on-Sea, Essex.

Another flake industry of Saale date is that found at High Lodge, Mildenhall. This industry consists mainly of scrapers of various different kinds, fashioned with extreme care, with resolved or step-flaking upon thick flakes struck out with a plain striking platform and a protruding bulb (i.e. formally to be classified as Clactonian flakes).

This industry seems likely to be an ancestor to the Quina Mousterian of the last Glaciation (see p. 60).

Tayacian[1] implements are smaller and lighter than Clactonian

[1] Named after the commune of Tayac in Central France.

but resemble them in other respects. At the cave of La Micoque in Central France they were found underlying advanced Acheulean hand-axes, and similar flakes were excavated from below Late Acheulean levels in the cave of Et-Tabun on Mount Carmel, Palestine.

THE CHOPPER CULTURES

In South-East Asia which lies outside the area covered by the Acheulean culture, such Lower Palaeolithic tools as are known have features in common which distinguish them from the hand-axe tradition. Specimens have been collected in North-West India, North-East China, Burma, Thailand, Malaya and Java.[1] They are all waterworn pebbles or rough lumps of rock (in Burma fossil wood) coarsely chipped at the edges from one or both sides so as to produce a rather blunt zig-zag working edge. These *choppers*, as they have been called, are more akin to the African pebble-tools than to pointed or ovate hand-axes. In China and India heavy flakes were also made without, or with very crude, retouch. They have been taken to represent a separate and contrasting cultural tradition. They show less uniformity than is found in the Acheulean.

THE ACHEULEAN CULTURE

The European type-sites of this culture are at Abbeville and at St Acheul, a suburb of Amiens, in North France. The Abbevillean (previously known as the Chellean)[2] is often treated as a distinct culture, but from all points of view, technique, tool-forms and

[1] The cultures are named respectively Soan (or Sohan), Choukoutienian, Anyathian, Fingnoan, Tampanian and Patjitanian. The Chinese implements are from caves at Chou K'un Tien near Peking, where remains of the primitive Sinanthropus pekinensis were found.

[2] From the name of another site, Chelles, a suburb of Abbeville, France.

45

chronological continuity, it is best regarded as the earliest phase of the Acheulean culture. The designation Chelles-Acheulean was at one time adopted in Africa. Wherever the culture is found, in South-West Europe and Britain, nearly all parts of Africa, in the Near East and South India, the characteristic tool shows astonishing uniformity in its development. This is the *hand-axe* (in French, *coup de poing*), an all-purpose tool, in which may be seen an effort towards standardization—the production of the ideal broken stone—rather than adaptation to various specific uses such as characterizes the Upper Palaeolithic stone equipment. There is a wide variety of types falling into two main series: pointed hand-axes in which one heavier end forms a butt, and more or less oval types (ovates) which have their centre of gravity near their middle and are trimmed to a thin edge on their whole circumference. Some characteristic outlines and their conventional names are shown in fig. 9. How far the variety of shapes answered to diversity of use it is not possible to say. Some have striking peculiarities. Often even the butt of a pointed hand-axe is so much sharpened by trimming that it is difficult to believe it was held in the hand, while the point is often so delicate as to seem too fragile for any use which the comparatively massive butt would suit. Some ovates are peculiarly unsuitable for holding in the hand in any position. Neither type as a class has any features which suggest hafting, although an occasional ovate is notched on either side as if for this purpose. Some of the later ovates, the 'twisted' type, have their edge curved in the form of a reversed S, and a very few in the form of a normal S, this being most likely a result of the working technique and not, as has been suggested, an ingenious device for improving the flight of the stone when used as a missile. The possibility that the ovates were thrown at the prey cannot of course be dismissed.

There is some evidence at Abbeville that early hand axes could belong to the Cromerian interglacial and a simple Abbevillian type of hand-axe has been recognized distinguished generally from those of the succeeding stages by the coarseness of the technique of manufacture. From the start pointed and ovate implements occur, usually varying from three to eight inches in length. The technical common denominator is that they all consist not of flakes, but of lumps of flint shaped by the removal of many small flakes. They are, to use the usual term, bifacial or core-implements. In making them flakes were struck off a large nodule or a large flake from all sides until it was reduced to the desired shape. Most of these flakes were discarded as wastage, though naturally a few of the better ones were themselves utilized as tools, with or without further trimming.

Early hand-axes have deep-biting scars left by flakes with prominent bulbs of percussion. Owing to the considerable concavity of the scars the edges have an uneven, approximately zig-zag line, and consequently the outline of the implement tends to be irregular. Experiment shows that this is the result obtained when a stone striker is used, or when flakes are removed by striking the whole piece against an immovable stone. These 'early' hand-axes are rarely finished by secondary retouch, i.e. finer flaking applied after the main shaping of the tool is completed. In the later stages of the culture, which flourish during the Hoxnian and continue in the last interglacial, more finely worked tools are believed to have been produced. The trimming flakes are much thinner, their bulbs of percussion shallower and more diffused, an effect probably achieved by using a striker of more resilient material, such as wood, bone or antler. The scars on the implements being much shallower and flatter and hence separated by less prominent ridges, combine to produce a smoother surface and, more important, straighter cutting-edges and a more regular outline. The area of surface removed by each trimming flake can now be increased without leaving an undesirably large negative bulb. Fig. 7 shows a hand-axe in the making. It has reached the stage of an advanced rough-out. The initial flaking may have been executed with a stone striker. The present object is to remove wide, shallow flakes in order to thin down the implement while leaving its faces as flat as possible. The flint is laid on the palm of the hand,

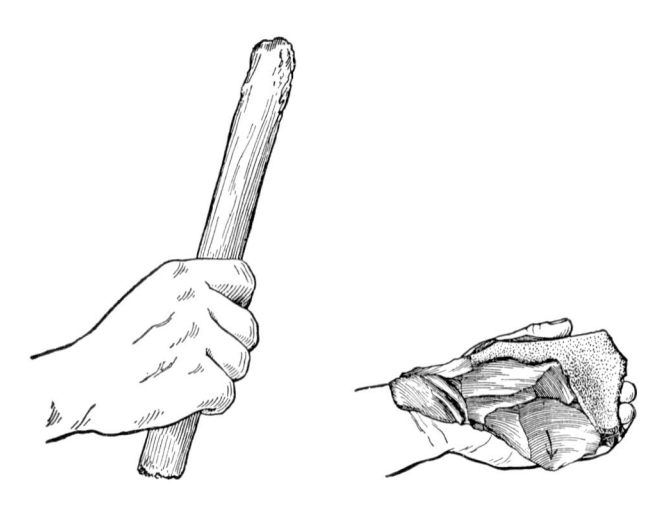

Fig. 7. A hand-axe in the making (cf. page 48). The hand-axe here illustrated, from the Middle Terrace gravels of the River Somme, near Amiens, N. France, is in fact an unfinished specimen apparently discarded by the flint worker because he was unable to remove a projecting knot which had formed on the side not shown in the figure. (*Scale* 1/5.)

the palm or the fingers in contact with the area from which the flake is to be struck. The edge of the flint (as indicated by the arrow) now receives the flaking blow from above with a wooden striker, and a thin flake is detached from the underside. Naturally the precise angle and the force required for the flaking blow is learned only by practice. It is doubtful if modern experimenters have ever achieved the neat regularity of the long and thin trimming flakes which were removed in fashioning Acheulean implements. The edges of these are often formed by a retouch so delicate as to suggest that a pressure technique like that described below in connexion with the Solutrean culture was already employed at this early date. Another method used to correct the irregularity of the edge of a tool, once the general outline was deemed satisfactory, was *step-flaking* (also called resolved flaking). Blows delivered directly on the point and edges removed tiny flakes terminated by hinge-fractures, the scars of which appear as a series of tiny steps on the margin of the tool (fig. 8).

Different standardized shapes of hand-axes were favoured at different times and in different regions, and through the immensely long duration of the culture, technique is gradually

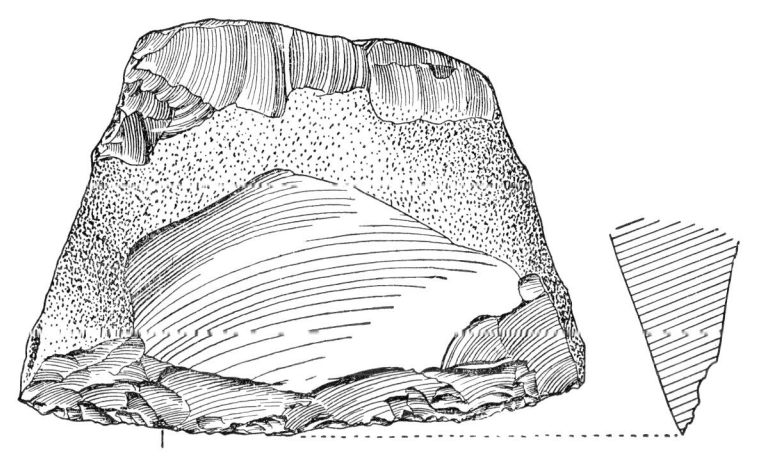

FIG. 8. Step- or resolved flaking on the cutting-edge of a Mousterian chopper from Le Moustier, Dordogne. (*Scale* 2/3.)

improved. Fig. 9 shows some of the leading types with their conventional names. There is, however, no chronological sequence of forms with universal validity. The hand-axe cultures show an evolution of technique and a variation of shapes and of the relative proportions of different shapes, but it is hardly possible to refer an implement with certainty to one of these stages on purely typological considerations. In fact the apparent typological distinctions described above cannot be proved at present in western Europe as the earliest Abbevillian stage has not been properly described. This stage is known from a small group of pits at Abbeville where the deposits containing hand-axes are claimed to belong to the Cromerian interglacial. No other comparably early groups of hand-axes have so far been recognized. A statistical

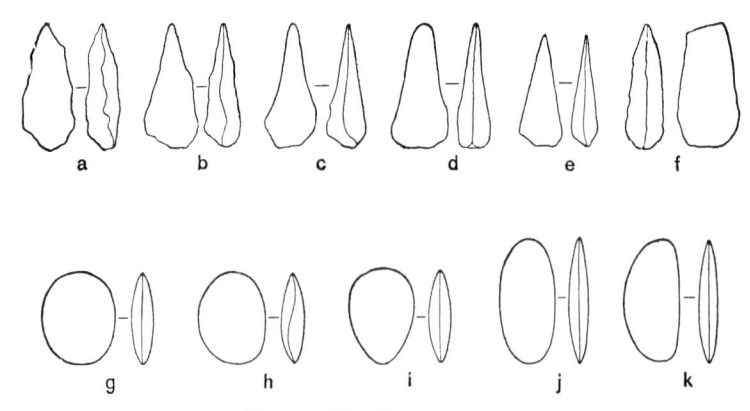

FIG. 9. Hand-axe types.

(*a—e*) Pointed hand-axes: (*a & b*) believed to be typical of Early Acheulean; (*c*) the 'ficron' (French for tip of a punt-pole); (*d*) lingulate (tongue-shaped), all typically Middle Acheulean; (*e*) Micoquian or lanceolate, characteristic of Late Acheulean; (*f*) cleaver, Middle Acheulean; (*g—k*) ovates: (*h*) the twisted ovate, is common in the English late-Middle Acheulean; (*i*) the cordate (heart-shaped) or Mousterian type; large specimens resembling (*j*) are sometimes called 'limandes' (French for flat-fish); and (*k*) is the amygdaloid (almond-shaped).

study of other groups of hand-axes tends to suggest that many groups of all dates have the supposedly early type of hand-axe (though in different proportions).

In England, typologically and geologically, only three stages of the hand-axe culture are generally distinguished. In the parish of Caversham, Berks, Early Acheulean pieces are found in gravels apparently earlier than the main Hoxnian aggradation, and possibly belonging to a short warm period separating two phases of the Lowestoft glaciation. However these occurrences like the supposedly earlier deposits at Abbeville must be viewed with suspicion. The earliest really certain Acheulian industry is that of the so-called middle stage, abundantly represented in the Hoxnian 100 ft. aggradation gravels of the Middle and Lower Thames, especially in the Swanscombe area of Kent. Here pointed and ovate hand-axe shapes continue, including a number of small sizes, the neat triangles and twisted ovates sometimes measuring as little as an inch and a half in length. In the Somme valley the Middle Acheulean has fewer ovates and a larger proportion of large pointed hand-axes. The late Acheulean of the Eemian interglacial is less clearly isolated in England than in France. Implements found overlying boulder clay at Gaddesden Row and in brick-earth overlying gravel at Wansunt on the Lower Thames may furnish examples of this stage. The old shapes continue, perhaps with an average reduction of size, while types such as the shiel-shaped (cordate) hand-axe and small elongated hand-axes with straight sides seem to be peculiar to the latest development. Cleavers, a rare type in Europe, but dominant in some stages of the South African sequences, occasionally occur in the Middle Acheulean of France and England. They have a broad straight cutting-edge set approximately at right-angles to the longer axis of the implement.

Acheulean flake-tools are less well known than they deserve to be owing to their neglect by the earlier collectors. Their shapes are irregular, but scrapers with carefully rounded edges and symmetrically pointed pieces occasionally occur. The retouch, generally confined to the margins, is similar to that used on the bifacial tools. Sometimes the flakes are clearly the by-product of hand-axe trimming, and no special technique seems to have been invented for producing flakes destined from the start for tool manufacture. In the European Acheulean as in that of South and East Africa, an independent Levallois flake technique develops within the later part of the hand-axe tradition (cf. Stellenbosch culture).

Although the main trend of Acheulean development was towards standardization, limited functional differences of the tools can be discerned: points and ovates, scrapers and cleavers. These variations we may suppose sprang from the four prime needs of a hunting and food-gathering community: weapons for chase; knives for dismembering the kill and cutting leaves and fruit; axes, knives and scrapers for working wood, bark and leather; and some sort of pointed implement for digging up edible roots. But many hand-axes could conceivably be used for all these tasks. The primitive Tasmanians seem to have regarded their chief stone tool—a thick roughly circular flake—as such an all-purpose implement.

Little can be said about the habitat of Acheulean man. He flourished in Europe principally in the Hoxnian and Eemian interglacials when the continent enjoyed a warm climate and harboured a fauna which included elephant and hippopotamus, rhinoceros, lion and the rare sabre-toothed tiger. Some cave sites with Acheulean implements are known in France and Palestine, but the vast majority of the implements are found on the surface of river gravels or imbedded in them. Even when allowance is made for displacement by river action and climatic effects, we still cannot avoid concluding that their makers haunted the banks of rivers and lakes. The skull fragments found in river gravel at Swanscombe have already been mentioned. The sharpness of many of the Acheulean hand-axes found in the Swanscombe gravels proves that they cannot have been transported far from the place where man abandoned them. At Olorgesailie in Kenya such a thick spread of hand-axes of the African Acheulean culture was found imbedded at various levels in lacustrine deposits that one must conclude that a succession of deserted workshops at this place had been ultimately covered by the nearby lake. At Caddington in Bedfordshire another Acheulean working floor was discovered in the last century, buried in the deposits of a small ancient lake. The finder collected the waste flakes left over from the manufacture of hand-axes and was able to fit many together, thus proving that they had lain undisturbed since the work was abandoned. In one case, after the flakes had been conjoined, it was even possible by pouring plaster of Paris into the central hollow to obtain a cast of the missing hand-axe. Another Acheulean lake-side settlement is at Toralba near Madrid. Here the presence of many elephants standing in the lake mud and evidence that they had been used as a food supply has led archaeologists to suppose that the elephants were driven into the lake and killed while trapped in the mud.

THE LEVALLOISIAN TECHNIQUE

A great advance in the manufacture of flake tools is seen in the Levalloisian, a technique so-named after an archaeological suburb of Paris. This is first recognized in Europe much later than the Clactonian, being found in France in deposits attributed to the local equivalent of the Saale glaciation, and thereafter recurs in different stages of evolution in the last interglacial and during the earlier part of the last glaciation. Different stages of the development of the technique are distinguishable according as large and broad flakes, or long, narrow blade-flakes were produced. It was for a long time thought that the Levallois technique was a separate flake culture, like the Clactonian but it is now recognized that this technique was an integral part of (late) Acheulean and later of Mousterian flint industries.

While it is untrue to say that the flakes were removed from Clactonian cores quite at random (for the flaking blows tended to move steadily round the circumference), yet the cores were not prepared beforehand for the removal of particular flakes. The Levalloisian method on the other hand was to trim the core carefully before the flake was struck off. In this way the shape of the eventual flake could be controlled to a considerable extent. The face of the core destined to form the back of the tool-flake was trimmed to an even, more or less flat surface, and from this prepared face the tool-flake was detached by delivering a blow on a striking platform worked on the edge of the core. For success it was essential to have the plane of this striking platform approximately at right-angles to the flatter core-face, and to ensure this a striking platform was carefully trimmed by the removal of small flakes. Consequently both the remnant of the striking platform on

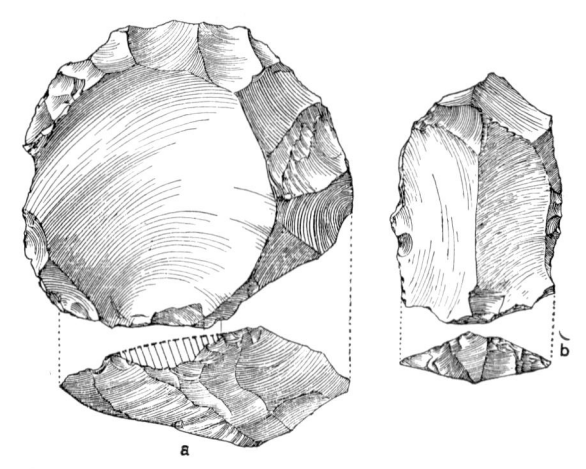

Fig. 10. Levalloisian core and flake. (*Scale* 1/3.)

(*a*) Top and end-view of a Levalloisian core from which a flake has been struck. The shading shows the part of the edge which, after striking, formed the faceted butt of the flake. (*b*) Levalloisian flake. The flake and core illustrated do not belong together, although they came from the same working floor in Cyrenaica, N. Africa.

the core and the butt of the tool-flake removed are 'faceted', i.e. present a number of small contiguous flake-scars. Flakes with faceted butts and the prepared cores from which they were struck are among the hallmarks of the Levalloisian technique. Fig. 10 shows examples of both. The cores tend towards a number of particular shapes, the commonest being sub-oval in outline and bun-shaped, having one face more domed than the other. They are known as *tortoise-cores*. The final shaping was executed by flaking directed alternately from both sides of the circular or oval edge, the flakes reaching to the centre of the flatter face, but on the domed side stopping short of the centre where cortex frequently remains. The flatter face has a central scar where the final tool-flake was removed. Once or twice a core and the very flake struck from it have been found together. The principal characteristic of

54

these flakes is the presence of a number of intersecting flake scars on the upper surface, the visible remains of the earlier trimming of the core.

It is curious that the prehistoric worker often expended almost as great care in shaping the underside of the tortoise core as the side from which the tool-flake came. Before it was struck the prepared core must in fact have resembled a clumsy hand-axe (though quite dissimilar from an Acheulean hand-axe), so that the Levalloisian technique can be regarded as the off-shoot of the hand-axe technology. The art of striking off a true Levallois flake from a tortoise core is certainly difficult and for many years no modern experimenter succeeded in reproducing the Levalloisian technique completely despite detailed knowledge of his methods. It is now generally recognized that this can be done only by raising the tortoise core in the hand and bringing it down on an anvil. Certain African and French research workers have successfully detached Levallois flakes in this manner. In the Levallois collections from Bakers Hole, Kent, we can observe the difficulties of the technique: a core left unstruck, no doubt owing to a flaw unrecognizable to a modern eye; flakes which have come off short or plunged into the core and brought away a lump at the end which rendered them useless as implements.

In the early stages Levalloisian tools are quite rough and shapeless, mere flakes whose sharp edges served for cutting and scraping without any further attention. As the tool-shapes became more specialized, in some cases in the direction of slender blade-like flakes and in others towards symmetrical points, the aim was still to produce the desired form as far as possible by an appropriate treatment of the core, so that when the flake was struck off it was ready for use as a tool without more ado. It is with this in mind that we must judge the skill of Levalloisian work. Tortoise cores naturally reflect the shapes of the tools they served to make: pointed cores for triangular points; rectangular rather elongated cores for blade-like flakes (which are sometimes struck from both ends of the core); approximately circular cores for broad flakes.

A peculiarity of some of the symmetrical points is the triple-curved Cupid's bow outline of the butts (in France this is called a 'chapeau de gendarme'). This happens when successive tool flakes are struck from the same position on the core: the second flake has the negative bulb of its predecessor above its own positive bulb. In the later stages of the culture the edges of these symmetrical points are frequently strengthened by trimming, but extensive retouch is rare. The later Levalloisian points seem intended for hafting as spear-heads, and they are probably the earliest implements to be mounted in this manner.

Of the seven stages of the Levalloisian dated by French workers on the geological evidence of the Somme valley, stage 4 belongs to the warm Eemian interglacial phase, but the earlier stages are found in deposits related to the Saale, and the later stages in deposits referred to the Weichsel glacial phases. Stages 3 and 4 have a large proportion of lighter and more blade-like flakes. Stages 1, 2 and 5 on the other hand produced large wide flakes. Stages 6 and 7 again have narrow flakes and neat triangular points, often retouched. All these stages we have recognized as belonging either to late Acheulean or Mousterian industries.

In England only two stages of the development of the technique can be clearly distinguished, and the dating of the earlier of these, represented by the working floor discovered at Baker's Hole, Northfleet, Kent, beneath Coombe Rock (a cold-phase deposit of sludged rock-rubble) is in dispute (see page 16). The phase undoubtedly corresponds with the Somme stage 5 (i.e. broad flakes with hand-axes), but the geological evidence favours a date in the Saale. It has been suggested that the industry is a local English variant of early Levalloisian which later emigrated to France, to be classified there as stage 5. The later English Levalloisian style is best exemplified by the implements found in brick-earth at Crayford, Kent, and at Creffield Road, Acton, London, which belong either to the last interglacial or to a warm phase during the last glaciation. The implements resemble those of the Somme stages 6 and 7.

In Africa it has always been recognized that the flake and the hand-axe techniques are closely welded in the same tradition. From the start hand-axes made on large flakes are not uncommon, and in the middle stages of the African Acheulean, flakes, sometimes of gigantic proportions, are regularly struck from cores with prepared platforms, i.e. by Levalloisian technique, and used to produce hand-axes and cleavers. Moreover, flake tools are an integral part of the culture, appearing first with smooth striking platforms and ultimately with faceted butts in the advanced Levalloisian manner. In the Near East, as in Europe, a great development of the use of Levallois techniques is found in association with the Mousterian culture in the Eemian interglacial, which we know in Syria and Palestine as Levallois-Mousterian industries for this reason.

THE SPREAD FROM AFRICA

The close analogies in the development of hand-axe cultures in Africa, Europe and Asia, and the apparent origin of these cultures from the pebble tool cultures of Africa has led to the suggestion that the Acheulean spread in successive waves from an African homeland. Its intermittent occurrence, both in Europe and in N.W. India during interglacials and its apparent disappearance during glacials lends support to such a theory.

The similarities between the Asiatic chopper tools and the African pebble tools have also led some to suggest that the former represent an early pre-hand-axe diffusion of culture from an African homeland, and that the primitive chopper cultures survived only in regions peripheral to the area of African culture diffusion. However, the extremely simple and crude form of these industries, and their lack of homogeneity might also indicate a separate centre or centres of origin in East Asia. The isolation of the early chopper tool cultures from the main hand-axe zones of influence led to local developments such as the flake culture of

Choukoutien, the Soan flake/chopper culture of North-West India and possibly the Clactonian culture of North-West Europe.

The dichotomy between the hand-axe cultures and the flake cultures of Europe is emphasized by their geographical distribution. Hand-axes are found principally in the lowland regions of S.W. Europe, bounded on the north and east by the Ardennes and the Alps. To the North and East of this region, particularly in Germany, flake cultures are almost exclusively found. A region of overlap occurs in Northern France, Belgium and South-East England, and there is here some evidence for contact between the two traditions in cultures.

The Levalloisian has been considered as a separate flake culture contemporary with the late Acheulean and to be the precursor of the Mousterian cultures. However, the close association between hand-axe and levallois techniques in Africa has led to a reappraisal of the European levalloisian. Although the association is less clear in Europe, classic levalloisian sites in Britain, such as Baker's Hole, contain some hand-axes and a proportion of flake tools which are not distinct from those found in Acheulean contexts. It is therefore more correct to consider the levalloisian as a specialized facies of the Acheulean tradition.

THE MOUSTERIAN CULTURE

The Mousterian culture of Europe flourished in the later part of the last interglacial and through the first phase of the last (weichsel) glaciation. Technologically the culture has roots in the two main traditions of the Lower Palaeolithic. Flakes are struck continuously from a discoid core (fig. 11), which ultimately becomes too small for further flaking and it is discarded. Normally individual flakes do not receive special attention prior to striking. The butts of large tool-flakes are usually faceted (generally more coarsely than in the Levalloisian), but those of the smaller flakes are almost invariably smooth. Trimming is normally

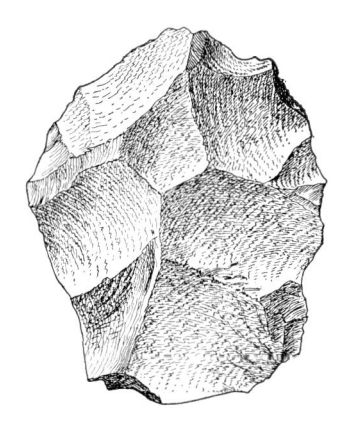

FIG. 11. Mousterian disc core from Devil's Tower cave, Gibraltar. (*Scale* 1/2.)

confined to the edges of the implement, rarely spreading over the back of the flake. The most characteristic piece is the point, possibly intended as a dart or spear-head. In a more evolved North African variant of the Mousterian, the Aterian culture, a true arrowhead appears, formed from a more or less coarsely trimmed flake, the retouch encroaching on the main flake surface only in the region of the tang, which is worked from both faces of the flake. These tanged points are the first certain evidence for the use of the bow. The Aterian equipment also includes flat points of narrow oval (laurel-leaf) outline. In Europe, however, the Mousterian has neither tanged nor leaf-shaped points, the former being unknown before the Gravettian culture of the Upper Palaeolithic and the latter appearing for the first time as the characteristic artifact of the Solutrean (see below, page 66). Mousterian industries everywhere comprise large numbers of side-scrapers with strong straight or curved working edges formed by skilled step-flaking. Many implements are intermediate in shape between the typical points and side-scrapers; some with one blunted and one sharper edge appear to be for use as knives, especially when the outline is quadrangular. From a side-scraper to a roughly fashioned knife the transition is gradual both in function and in tool-form. The hand chopper is another typical Mousterian tool. It is generally oval or oblong, one longer edge being thick and blunt (consisting often of cortex) and the other sharpened by trimming on both faces. Whenever the depth of deposit in a cave enables one to survey Mousterian implements over a long period, the earlier stages show a ruder technique than the later, but the type-tools remain the same. In addition to these a hand-axe of late Acheulean type is frequently included, while late Mousterian industries occasionally include coarse burins (page 63) and blades.

The Mousterian in Europe has been found, as a result of excavations and statistical studies carried out in France, to be divided into a number of different industrial styles or cultures. The principal facies are the Standard Mousterian, the Quina Mousterian, the Ferrasie Mousterian, the Denticulate Mousterian and the Mousterian of Acheulean tradition. Many of these stone industries are characterized by the proportion of Levallois flakes, or the proportion of hand-axes found in a statistical sample of the industry, the proportion of hand-axes being especially high in the *Mousterian of Acheulean Tradition*. The traditional type of Mousterian is referred to above as the *Standard Mousterian*. The *Quina Mousterian* contains very fine step retouched scrapers on extremely thick flakes, and the *Denticulate Mousterian* is characterized by an overwhelming proportion of small flakes with single notches or multiple denticulations. All these industries appear at the time of writing to be separate cultural manufactures. At the cave of Combe Grenal in Western France, these industries regularly replace one another at intervals throughout a long period covering the Eemian and the earlier part of the last Glaciation.

The Quina Mousterian can with fair certainty be attributed to a distinct human type, its characteristic implements having been found in undisturbed cave deposits along with bones of the primitive Neanderthal man, *Homo neanderthalensis*. The succeeding cultures are associated in western Europe with men of the modern type, *Homo sapiens,* as are certain other forms of Mousterian cultures. After their arrival no further trace of Neanderthal man is found.

Only meagre traces of the Mousterian have been found in Britain. A typical industry with points and choppers is known from Kent's Cavern, Torquay, Devon. Another Mousterian industry, very similar to those found in Western France, was found on the hillside below a Rock Shelter on Oldbury Hill, near Ightham, Kent. The only physical remains of *Homo neanderthalensis* so far discovered in the British Isles are some molars excavated in 1911 in a cave on St Brelade bay on the island of Jersey. They were accompanied by Mousterian flint implements and bones of woolly rhinoceros.

THE BLADE TECHNIQUE

Following the Mousterian in western Europe are found a succession of cultures grouped under the term Upper Palaeolithic which bring the story from the second weichsel interstadial (i.e. the warmer spell between the second and third subdivisions of the last glaciation) down to the final retreat of the ice from Europe at the end of the Pleistocene, about 10,000 years ago. These cultures are all recognized by the use of the blade technique in their flint industry, a technique first adopted as an industrial style in North Africa (Cyrenaica) and the Syrian-Palestine coast line in the Eemian interglacial and presumed to have spread by diffusion or culture-contact into west Europe.

All the Upper Palaeolithic cultures are alike in their concentration on blade-production, in which they contrast with their Mousterian predecessors. The blades are long, narrow flakes with approximately parallel sides, struck directly from the core, which frequently assumes the shape of a fluted truncated cone (fig. 12). No individual preparation was required for the blades, but the

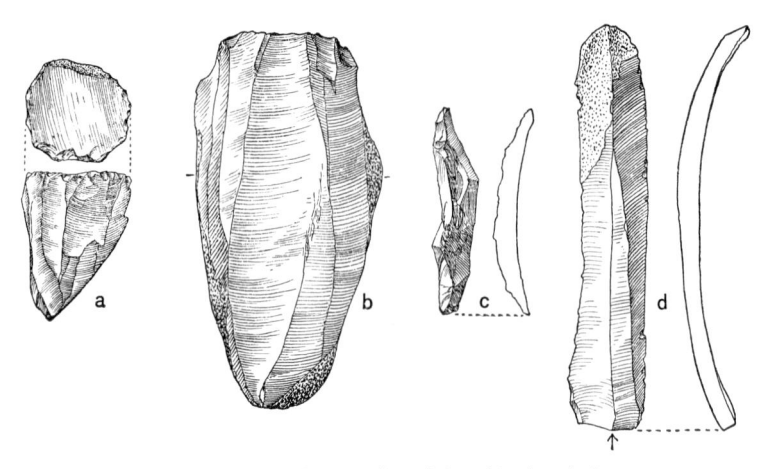

FIG. 12. Blade cores and rejuvenating flake. (*Scale* 1/2.)

(*a*) and (*b*) blade cores; (*c*) rejuvenating flake struck from the flaking edge of a large blade core in order to improve the direction of flaking, showing the scars of blades already removed; (*d*) a typical well-controlled blade. (*b*), (*c*) and (*d*) are from La Madeleine, the type-site of the Magdalenian culture.

striking platform on the core had to be periodically renewed, and the flake removed in doing this is another hall-mark of the technique. The removal of long thin blades probably required the use of a punch of wood, bone or antler, the point of which could be accurately placed on the relatively small area of the striking platform. Some details of the process may be surmised from eye-witness accounts of the manufacture of long flint or obsidian blades by American Indians in historical times. One such account was published in 1885. The punch was a stick between 2 and 3 inches in diameter and from two and a half feet to four feet long, having at one end a pointed tip of bone or antler. For some kinds of work the tips were scraped to a rather blunt point, for others, left with a slightly rounded end about half an inch in diameter. If the work was done seated, the core was embedded in hard earth and held by the feet, and the shorter flaking staff was used. Sometimes the core was firmly bound between strips of wood, on which the knapper stood while operating with the longer staff. The latter was held in both hands, the upper end against the chest. The point was placed in a prepared indentation on the squared edge of the core and a blade removed by sudden pressure. The work was divided among the tribe, some specializing in preparing the quadrangular cores and chipping the indentation for the point of the staff.

In all blade industries many blades were utilized as struck, and the formed implements which are made the basis of cultural distinctions are usually a minority of the artifacts. The principal flint tools of the Upper Palaeolithic are the knife with blunted back, the end-scraper and the burin or graver, nearly all formed on thin blades. It is arguable that some of the blunted-back blades served as arrow tips, but others are clearly intended for cutting. The nature of the burin is best understood from the illustrations on Plate VII. It usually has a narrow edge, variously formed at right angles to the plane of the flake, adapted to working and engraving antler and bone, both materials being used in the manufacture of points and harpoons and in artistic carving.

THE UPPER PALAEOLITHIC IN WESTERN EUROPE

With the arrival of the use of the blade technique Upper Palaeolithic Stone industries (which were often largely composed of tools for making other tools or weapons, i.e. of bone or wood) became progressively subject to local differentiation. It is not possible in this manual to describe all the many different cultures and industries of Africa, Asia and Europe. Here and in the succeeding Neolithic section we contain ourselves to describing the local succession in Britain and France.

THE EARLY PERIGORDIAN CULTURE

The characteristic implements are comparatively wide blades blunted along one edge by the removal of small chips at a right angle or steeply inclined to the main plane. These appear to be knives, although the smaller and narrower examples may well have served as arrow or javelin points. End-scrapers and *bec de flûte* and angle burins (see Plate VII) are numerous. Bone is used only for roughly fashioned points.

THE AURIGNACIAN CULTURE

The development of the Perigordian in Central France was interrupted by the arrival from without of the Aurignacian culture, which lacks blunted-back blades and has scrapers and burins of distinctive types. The nosed scraper, with domed back and working edge neatly rounded by 'fluted' trimming—the removal of narrow parallel flakes—is common. The distinctive Aurignacian burin on the other hand is relatively rare. The shape is best appreciated from Plate VII. This *burin busqué* (convex burin) is not a burin in the normal sense, but a special form of the nosed scraper.

Another Aurignacian type is a thickish blade with rounded ends, trimmed around the whole edge and slightly constricted at the centre, in outline approximating to a figure of eight. Hafted bone points were specially favoured by the Aurignacian hunters. One very distinctive type with a rounded base split by a deep V-shaped incision along the major axis of the flattened oval section, is said to be characteristic of the earliest stage of the culture found in France, and to be followed by other forms without the basal incision, in which the section becomes gradually more circular and the original oval or slightly lozenge-shaped outline becomes narrower.

THE PERIGORDIAN CULTURE

The Upper Perigordian or Gravettian, which is found overlying the Aurignacian in cave sites, is related to the Early Perigordian or Châtelperronian, of which it appears to be a refined and evolved descendant. Its blunted-back blades are more regular in outline and trimming, and frequently much narrower. The back, which in the Châtelperronian tends to be curved, is now straight, turning sharply to slope obliquely to the point. A later stage of the Gravettian is distinguished by the possession of points prepared for hafting by a single-shouldered or double-shouldered tang, the latter known from a site as Font Robert points.

The clear affinity between the Châtelperronian and the Gravettian has led to their grouping by several workers under a single title, the Perigordian culture. This theory regards the Gravettian as evolved from the Châtelperronian in Central France, the evolution continuing contemporaneously with and close alongside the Aurignacian which intruded at the end of the Châtelperronian stage. This last is designated Perigordian I. Perigordian II (small blunted-back blades and broader blades truncated and blunted obliquely at the point) is a broader development from I and is contemporary with stages of the earliest Aurignacian. The earlier and later Gravettian stages become Perigordian IV and V.[1] An industry which was formerly believed to be intermediary between the Châtelperronian and Gravettian (old Perigordian III) is now more generally accepted as phase VI of the Gravettian. The intermediate stages between the Châtelperronian and Gravettian are not clearly represented and the relationship between these two cultures may not be as straightforward as was formerly believed. The advocates of this division argue six stages of the Aurignacian culture distinguishing them by the forms of bone points. Their correspondence in time with various stages of the Perigordian seems to require further confirmation. Blades treated like Châtelperronian knives are found alongside the final Acheulean in Syria and Palestine, whereas industries resembling the Gravettian, both with and without tanged points, have been

[1] The famous painted cave at Lascaux, at Montignac, Dordogne, has been claimed by the advocates of the Perigordian theory as the work of Perigordian artists; it is now generally regarded as early Magdalenian.

found at sites stretching across Central Europe and reaching to the Don basin. This evidence of differing distribution is generally interpreted in support of the old view (i.e. in opposition to the Perigordian theory) that France experienced successive culture-bearing invasions from separate centres of evolution as yet unidentified. The distribution of Aurignacian sites is again distinct, following approximately the mountainous country from Transcaucasia to the Alps. The prey of all these Palaeolithic hunters was principally mammoth and horse, and their camps were sometimes sited to intercept these animals on their seasonal migration routes. Both Aurignacians and Gravettians have left paintings on cave-walls in France. The Gravettians are also famous for their female figurines of mammoth ivory and soft rocks. They have been found in most areas where the culture occurs. The small animal figurines are less widely distributed.

THE SOLUTREAN CULTURE

In the Solutrean culture which supervenes on the Gravettian, the best tools are *pressure-flaked* and have a very distinctive appearance, while the accompanying end-scrapers, burins and untrimmed flakes do not differ essentially from those of earlier and later Upper Palaeolithic cultures. The new pressure technique resembles the blade technique described on page 61, but it is applied on a smaller scale. Small flat flakes are removed by pressing against the edge of the primary flake with a hard point. By this means the retouch is extended over a much wider area of the implement than was hitherto possible. The retouch from the two edges covers the whole surface, which is left with neat fluted scars. The most characteristic forms on which the pressure technique was employed—in the early stages on one face and later on both—were points with outlines resembling a laurel or willow leaf. The British Museum possesses one masterpiece of laurel-leaf shape which measures 11 in. × $2\frac{1}{2}$ in. and is less than $\frac{1}{4}$ in. thick. In the later Solutrean are found pressure-flaked arrowheads with a single shoulder or a proper tang for hafting; and the recently excavated site of Parpalló in Valencia, Spain, has produced barbed-and-tanged Solutrean arrowheads hardly distinguishable from the type used in Britain and Europe in the Bronze Age. Whereas the origin of the Solutrean was once sought in South-East Europe, where in Hungarian caves a primitive Solutrean was said to occur, the Spanish discovery suggests on the contrary that it may have reached France through Spain from North Africa, where the Aterian culture (pages 59, 60) had tanged and leaf-shaped points. The Gravettian and Font Robert points show that Europe knew the bow before the Solutreans reached France, but we need no longer assume that the latter adopted it from their Gravettian predecessors. The Solutrean horse-hunters made no distinguished use of bone and antler, but practised an advanced art of stone sculpture in high relief depicting processions of animals.

THE MAGDALENIAN CULTURE

The succeeding culture, the Magdalenian, reflects the well integrated society and economy of communities of fishers and reindeer-hunters. In it the working of reindeer antler assumed an even greater importance than hitherto. Consequently burins figure still more prominently in the equipment, the 'parrot's beak' type being an addition to the earlier varieties and peculiar to the Magdalenian culture. The end-scrapers are not distinctive, nor the large quantities of untrimmed blades, although among the latter occasional specimens of marvellous length and thinness show that perfection had been attained in the technique. Blades with blunted backs occur, and in the earlier stages were manufactured in diminutive sizes, as small as half an inch long and one-eighth of an inch wide. In these *microliths* we see the beginning of a tool tradition which came to dominate in some cultures of the Mesolithic period.[1] They are believed to have been used

[1] Their manufacture in large numbers is also a feature of the later stages of the blade industries in North Africa (Capsian). Microlithic stone industries

singly or in pairs to barb wooden points (which have not survived) or hafted in rows to form a composite cutting or sawing edge. The Magdalenian appears to have lasted longer in Western Europe than the preceding cultures of the Upper Palaeolithic, probably surviving to the end of the Pleistocene. It is subdivided into six stages according to characteristic forms of antler points and harpoons:

Magd. I	Points with wide bevelled bases which are roughened for hafting by incised lines.
Magd. II	Points with narrower bevelled bases or pointed conical bases and shafts of circular section.
Magd. III	Smaller points with bevelled bases, often having single or double longitudinal grooves on the shaft.
Magd. IV	Harpoons with rudimentary unilateral barbs.
Magd. V	Harpoons with long unilateral barbs.
Magd. VI	Harpoons with long bilateral barbs.

The apogee of Magdalenian art, in both painting and engraving of cave walls and the carving of antler, is reached in stage IV, to which period the famous painted caves of Altamira and Font de Gaume belong.

THE UPPER PALAEOLITHIC IN BRITAIN

Upper Palaeolithic culture is only sparsely represented in Great Britain, and was nowhere wholly identical with the cultures of Central France. The Châtelperronian is wholly unknown. Kent's Cavern, near Torquay, Devon, contained impoverished versions

---

producing implements closely resembling those of prehistoric Europe and Africa have been found in Central India, Ceylon and Australia. The Indian microliths continued in use at least until the beginning of the Christian era. Geometric shapes were favoured in hunting communities, while food-producing communities made chiefly blades. In south-east Australia microliths were being made by the aborigines when white settlement began, but were abandoned soon afterwards for iron.

of Aurignacian and Magdalenian (unilaterally and bilaterally barbed harpoons) separated by coarsely pressure-flaked pieces declared to be 'proto-Solutrean'. The cave of Ffynnon Beuno in the Vale of Clwyd produced a burin busqué (Aurignacian) and a proto-Solutrean piece. The nearby cave of Cae Gwyn had an Aurignacian nosed-scraper in a deposit overlain at one place by boulder clay believed to correspond to the second glacial phase of the weichsel, suggesting thus a dating similar to that of the French Aurignacian. In the Paviland cave in the Gower Peninsula, Aurignacian burins and nosed-scrapers were found and—unfortunately without a valid stratigraphic separation blunt back blades and a tanged point akin to the Gravettian. From the caves of Creswell Crags in Derbyshire a better Gravettian-type industry known as the *Creswellian* has been excavated. In Robin Hood's Cave there is a 'proto-Solutrean' industry; but the richest deposits, in Mother Grundy's Parlour, have a Creswellian industry developing through a long period, the blunted-back blades diminishing in size until microlithic proportions are reached. This local evolution reflects the cultural isolation of Britain at this period. The industries of the Mendip caves seem to show a similar provincial development. Here a bilaterally barbed harpoon from Aveline's Hole is a good Magdalenian type, but on the whole only a remote contact with that culture can be assumed. Only the scantiest traces of artistic activity have been found in the British cultures of this period. A horse's head engraved on bone from Creswell Crags, is, however, comparable to Magdalenian work in quality though different in style.

THE MESOLITHIC OF EUROPE

Magdalenian culture, the closest adaptation of hunting economy to sub-arctic climatic conditions, is no longer found in Europe after the beginning of the milder post-glacial period. The Hamburgian culture of North-West Germany—in spite of its distinctive burin, tanged arrowhead and 'thong-cutter' of antler, and its lack of harpoons—appears to afford a last glimpse of the heirs of the Magdalenian tradition as they moved in the tracks of the northward migrating reindeer close in the wake of the retreating ice. The cultures, termed Mesolithic, which occupy the period between the withdrawal of the ice and the first appearance of agricultural and stock-raising communities, have a different stamp, and in Europe at least they mark a break with the past. Two factors determine the complex picture they present. As forest grew over Europe again, the descendants of the indigenous Palaeolithic population were obliged to adapt themselves to a new environment. The great gregarious animals hunted by their ancestors had departed or become extinct, and the methods of the hunt had to be modified for the pursuit of forest game: ox, red deer, elk, wild pig, beaver, etc. The other factor was the arrival in Europe, as the climate improved, of people bearing a culture evolved in North Africa. Mesolithic tribesmen were still food-gatherers. Some communities were confined to the sea-coast on the edge of the forest, and there fished and collected shell-fish. Others depended more on hunting and adapted themselves to a forest life. Others again—the heirs of a North African industrial tradition—sought out the forest-free areas of the interior. To a varying degree in each case their material equipment is developed from elements already present in the Upper Palaeolithic. The principal tools are of flint, and while antler and bone tools are also made, the stimulus and ability to carve these materials artistically have, like the pictorial art of the Upper Palaeolithic, quite vanished. All Mesolithic cultures include scrapers and borers of various shapes, frequently burins and always many untrimmed but utilized flakes. The most striking characteristics, however, of the majority of the cultures is the inclusion of a varying proportion of the tiny implements called *microliths*, of irregular or geometric shapes according to the tradition, designed for mounting as boring and cutting tools. Singly they formed the barbs or points of wooden or bone arrows (and no doubt fish-hooks also) and mounted in series they combined to form a cutting-edge. The presence of a microlithic tendency in the Magdalenian and its dominance in the final Palaeolithic of North Africa was referred to on page 49.

In Britain four divisions of mesolithic culture can be recognized, and we confine our attention to these. One is native, the survival of the insular Upper Palaeolithic tradition. The other three are branches of the mesolithic cultures of the Continent.

The culture of the native Mesolithic, derived from the British Upper Palaeolithic, is best represented in the higher levels at Creswell Crags, Derbyshire. In the upper layers the microlithic tendency, noticeable already in an earlier stage, predominates, but the tools are irregular and show lack of skill in workmanship.

The Maglemose Culture of Great Britain is an intrusive western extension of a culture native in Denmark and the Baltic, which probably travelled to England across fen country now submerged by the North Sea. The flint equipment of these peoples is best known from excavations at Broxbourne, Herts. They dwelt on the borders of streams and lakes, in the heart of the forest, and fished with barbed and notched harpoon-heads of bone. Their flint tools consist of round scrapers and end-scrapers formed on blades struck from conical cores, untrimmed flakes, microliths of non-geometric shapes, and some heavy axes. The last are an interesting reflection of the requirements of the forest environment, being without precedent in the Upper Palaeolithic stone equipment. One type is a core-axe, and the other is made from a flake. An elongated version of the core-axe is known as the Thames pick from its being commonly found in dredging that river. Although they too inhabited the forest, the Creswellians produced no stone axes for dealing with timber. However most Creswellian sites are on high ground which was never very thickly wooded.

A particularly early version of the Maglemose Industry is that found at Star Carr in Yorkshire, dated to around 7000 B.C. Here, the barbed points, originally called harpoons by archaeologists but since shown to be spearheads mostly used for fish spears, are made of antler and not bone. The site is of great interest to archaeologists because it was preserved by immersion in boggy gravel and in addition to flint implements and stone beads, barbed antler points and a whole range of antler implements were preserved together with their debris of manufacture, and also the wooden platform on which the hunters were living at the lake side.

Another particularly earlier Mesolithic culture in Britain is that called the Sauveterrian after the site of Le Martinet, Sauveterre-le-Lemance in Western France. The flint tools which identify this culture consist of a number of varieties of very small (microlithic) blunted backed blades. Sauvetterian sites are mainly found around the coasts in the highland region of Britain, i.e. in Wales, Cornwall and Yorkshire.

In North Africa, the Upper Palaeolithic tendency to reduce flint blades to microlithic size led finally to standardized geometric forms. It is possible, therefore, that the Tardenoisian culture found in Spain, France, Belgium, Britain, South and Central Germany, Poland and Russia, and characterized by the same geometric shapes, was introduced into Europe by tribes forced to leave Africa through the desiccation of the Sahara at the close of the European ice-age. Tardenoisian immigrants spread over England, Wales and Scotland, but apparently not Ireland. They kept to forest-free areas, sandy soils or rocky places at high altitudes, settling thickly on the sand country of South-East England and South-West Scotland. They seem to have reached Britain in two waves, the first using small blunted-back blades of regular but not geometric proportions, and a second wave characterized by geometric microliths: trapezes, crescents, triangles. The wooden hafts on which the microliths were mounted have all perished, but there is satisfactory evidence of such mounting. A tiny triangle of flint was found imbedded in a vertebra of a human Tardenoisian skeleton excavated in the island of Téviec, off the south-west coast of Brittany; at Vig in eastern Denmark was found the skeleton of an aurochs slain by an arrow similarly

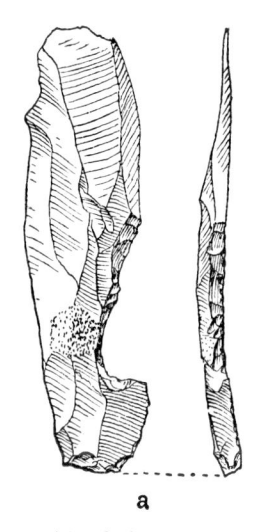

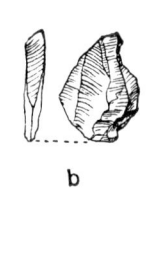

FIG. 13. (a) Blade notched for making a microlith; (b) Microburin; respectively from Peacehaven, Sussex, and Manton Warren, Lincolnshire. (*Scale* 1/1.)

tipped; and below peat at White Hill, near Huddersfield, thirty-five microlithic flints were found in a row so as to suggest that they had been mounted in a handle long since perished.

A constant component of Tardenoisian industries is the microburin, so-called from its supposed resemblance in miniature to the burins of the Upper Palaeolithic. The purpose of these pieces puzzled archaeologists for long, but they now seem to be satisfactorily explained: to make a geometric microlith a beginning was made by working a notch at the centre of a blade, which was then broken at the constriction (fig. 13). The rejected fragment, the microburin, is a piece of wastage and not an implement. The microburin technique is encountered in other microlithic cultures besides the Tardenoisian, e.g. in the Maglemosian of northern Europe and Britain.

The fourth category of Mesolithic culture in Britain is found at coastal sites in western Scotland, in caves near Oban, and on the sandy shore of Oronsay. The flint equipment has degenerated because of the scarcity of the raw material, the blades and scrapers making a poor comparison with other microlithic industries. There are no implements suited to a forest life. The Scottish Mesolithic people kept to the coast, fished, gathered shell-fish, and hunted seals, deer, boar, badger and wild cat. Characteristic tools are elongated pebbles, chosen for their shape, whose battered ends betray usage, but whether this usage was the prising of shell-fish from rocks, or as 'fabricators' in working flint—both have been suggested—remains uncertain.

In Northern Ireland an entirely distinct native tradition is seen in the flints of the Larnian culture, which are found derived in the raised beach of the Litorina transgression (see Chronological Table III, footnote). Here neither axes nor microliths were made. A coarse pick-like tool is the most characteristic type.

EARLY FARMING CULTURES

About 5400 years ago, the first farming and stock-raising communities reached Britain. Here, as everywhere, the technique of food-production which they introduced altered human life as never before. Released from the passive dependence on nature of the hunter and food-gatherer, men began to plan their economy by controlling the forces of nature. It has already been pointed out that in the Neolithic cultures of Europe by the middle of the second millennium B.C. many items of their equipment echo the higher metal-using cultures of the Mediterranean. Outside the Mediterranean area, however, the difficulties of obtaining supplies of copper and especially of tin, their high cost, and no doubt also the secretiveness of the early metallurgists, prevented a rapid spread of metal-working. Communities familiar with metal tools through the rare traded specimens which reached them were compelled to retain their stone equipment. One result of this was that they tried to copy the new metal tools in their traditional material. The shapes of the earliest metal tools had been based on those of stone types, and now some specific characters of metal forms, such as the splaying blade produced by hammering, are transferred to stone. The flint dagger of Denmark and the stone battle-axes found over almost the whole of Europe are the most striking examples of this process. Even the practice of grinding and polishing stone tools, which is a regular feature of Neolithic cultures, may have been in the first place an attempt to imitate metal prototypes. It is not known where the grinding and polishing of stone originated.

Towards the end of the fourth millennium B.C. Neolithic farmers spread to well drained soils over much of south and eastern England, east Scotland and north-east Ireland. They built ditched camps on hilltops and buried their dead in long barrows. All the neolithic communities made use of chipped and ground stone axes of various shapes. No doubt the special usefulness of these tools lay in clearing forest for agricultural land, and in preparing heavy timbers for building the houses required by the relatively settled conditions of agricultural life. Some of these tools may have been in fact the heads of hoes used in tillage. They were either chipped to their final shape, or after chipping ground smooth by rubbing on a flat sandstone surface. The lustre of some specimens, particularly those made of greenstone (and probably intended as ritual objects), suggests that a finer abrasive was sometimes used. Flint and igneous rock were the principal materials. Within certain limits there is a great variety of shapes, but it is not yet possible to arrange these in the chronological order of their appearance or even to define types peculiar to different cultural groups.

There is evidence that the exploitation of igneous rocks for axes was organized over great distances. The igneous rock of Penmaenmawr (see page 24 above) was worked in regular factory sites on the mountain side and the roughly chipped products were distributed southwards as far as Wiltshire, the final grinding and polishing being left apparently to the customers. Another such factory site was recently discovered in Great Langdale, Cumberland. Cornish greenstone was distributed over South-West England. Flint was no doubt obtained from local sources when they were available, though flint mines such as those at Grimes Graves in Norfolk and Cissbury in Sussex supplied implements of fresh flint to a wide area. The Grimes Graves mines are dated between 2400 and 1600 B.C. (by radio-carbon dating) and the Cissbury mines around 3000 B.C.

Different forms of arrowhead were used by different groups of early Neolithic farmers. Some groups had a leaf-shaped or lozenge-shaped type, made by pressure-trimming on a thin flake while other groups inherited from their Mesolithic ancestry a transverse type of arrowhead intended for mounting on the shaft with the broad, sharp edge to the front. Birds are brought down more quickly by such an arrow, which is also less liable to be lost through imbedding itself in tree-tops. The wide distribution and frequency of finds of arrowheads is a reminder of the continued importance of hunting in Neolithic times.

The remaining flint equipment of the Windmill Hill Neolithic is not very impressive, consisting of end- and side-scrapers and numerous rather shapeless flakes without trimming. One rare but distinctive implement, a flint sickle, which appears to be Neolithic in Britain, is usually skilfully flaked on both faces. Whether its principal use was to harvest crops or to cut leaves as fodder is debatable. Also characteristic of the middle Neolithic in East Anglia is a large projectile point known as a 'laurel-leaf'.

The first metal-users in England belong to the Beaker Culture, which reached this country from the coast of Brittany and the region of the Lower Rhine about 1900 B.C. How far these people introduced their own metallurgical industry or imported their bronze from Ireland, where the manufacture of bronze implements began at about the same period, remains uncertain. The Beaker people buried their dead in trench graves or in boxes constructed of stone slabs, often under round barrows, and they are further distinguished by their pottery and by the flint and bronze daggers which were sometimes placed in their graves. Probably metal was still a luxury for them and they still relied largely on flint and stone for their ordinary tools. In flint they made neat barbed-and-tanged arrowheads and skilful imitations of bronze daggers. Their stone battle-axes may also ultimately be imitations of metal prototypes. Also of Beaker type is the polished-edge blade knife, a long blade with one edge polished, whose use has not been precisely determined.

Another tool which may have been used by the Rinyo-Clacton people is the *discoidal knife,* the shape of which may vary from circular through oval and triangular to oblong. It consists of a large thin flake of flint, with an edge sharpened by polishing. The faces may be polished or left as they were flaked. The *slug-knife,* in which one face, the main flake surface, is left unworked, appears to be an appurtenance of the Food Vessel culture, which occupies the later part of the Early Bronze Age in Northern England and Scotland. Since our Early Bronze Age invaders fused with rather than superseded the pre-existing Neolithic population, it is not surprising that the Neolithic leaf-shaped type of arrowhead overlaps in time with the barbed-and-tanged type. Many of the stone axes found on the surface of our fields must belong to the Early Bronze Age. The use of flint scrapers and untrimmed flakes continued through the whole of the Bronze Age, and examples may even be found on Iron Age sites. Typical Early Bronze Age scrapers are more or less round and trimmed with very fine and regular pressure-flaking. The greater part of the nondescript flint flakes and implements taken from the surface of fields, particularly from the ploughed downlands of southern England where they are specially common, are of Neolithic or Bronze Age date, though even in the case of finished implements such as scrapers it may be uncertain to which period they belong. Rough flakes are often undatable. The difficulties of classifying some of these common types result from their being found scattered on the surface without other datable associated objects, and without the evidence of relative dating which stratified finds would give. Some of the implements mentioned above have been attributed to a culture phase only by noting the coincidence of their distribution with the known distribution of the culture as a whole. The perforated stone mace-head is an example of a poorly dated type. It was possibly known to the Windmill Hill peoples (who probably inherited it from the local Mesolithic), and it was certainly made in the Bronze Age. Sometimes the perforation is narrower in the middle than at the mouth on either side ('hour-glass' perforation). In this case it seems that the perforation was effected by rotating a stick in wet sand within a cavity on either face, or by pecking at the stone from both sides with a hard point. Other (and apparently later) mace-heads, axe-hammers and battle-axes, have a straight-sided perforation. Here a hollow cylindrical borer of bone or metal must have been used.

The cultural affinities of these and other flint and stone implements found in Britain associated with cultures of the later prehistoric period are described in greater detail in the museum handbook dealing with the period.

SELECT BIBLIOGRAPHY

Palaeolithic Archaeology is a changing subject. The works listed below include the principal monographs in this field in 1967, and also a number of works of interpretation. Dr West's work *Pleistocene Geology and Biology*, and Professor Clark's *Prehistoric Europe: The Economic Basis* may be recommended as up-to-date and important studies of this kind. A number of older works such as those by Reginald Smith, Worthington G. Smith and Sir John Evans are mentioned because they include drawings and descriptions of specimens in the Museum's collection. The useful series of popular introductions published by the Natural History Museum are also listed. A bibliography covering the latest periods in which flint was in general use in Europe, after the introduction of farming, will be found in the companion volume in this Museum, Mr Brailsford's *Later Prehistoric Antiquities of the British Isles*.

Biberson, P. *Le Cadre Paléogéographique de la Préhistoire du Maroc Atlantique*. Pub. du Service des Antiq. du Maroc. Fasc. 16. Rabat 1961
Bordes, F. *Typologie du Paléolithique ancien et moyen*. Memoire I Pub. de L'Inst. de Préhistoire de l'Université de Bordeaux 1961
Bordes, F. *Les Limons Quaternaires du Bassin de la Seine*, Inst. Pal. Humaine Archives mem. 26, n d.
Brailsford, J. W. *Later Prehistoric Antiquities of the British Isles*. British Museum, London 1963
Butser, K. *Environment and Archaeology*. London 1965
Caton-Thompson, G. *Kharga Oasis in Prehistory*. London 1952
Clark, J. D. *The Prehistoric Cultures of the Horn of Africa*. Cambridge 1954
Clark, J D. *The Prehistory of Southern Africa*. London 1959
Clark, J. D. *Kalambo Falls*. In Press 1967
Clark, J. G. D. *The Mesolithic Age in Britain*. Cambridge 1932
Clark, J. G. D. *The Mesolithic Settlement of Northern Europe*. Cambridge 1936
Clark, J. G. D. *Prehistoric Europe: The Economic Basis*. Glos. 1952
Clark, J. G. D. *Star Carr*. Cambridge 1954
Clark, J. G. D. *World Prehistory*. Cambridge 1961
Clark, Sir Wilfred le Gros. *History of the Primates, an Introduction to the study of fossil man*. British Museum (Natural History) London 1949
Clark, Sir Wilfred le Gros. *The Antecedents of Man*, 2nd Edn. Edinburgh 1962
Cole, Sonia. *The Neolithic*. British Museum (Natural History) 1961
Cole, Sonia. *The Prehistory of East Africa*, 2nd Edn. London 1964
Efimenko, P. P. *Kostienki I*. Moscow (Academy of Sciences S.S.R. Archaeological series. Vol 88) 1954
Evans, Sir John. *The Ancient Stone Implements of Great Britain*. London 1897 (2nd Edn.)
Felgenhauer, F. *Willendorf in der Wachau*
Garrod, D. A. E. *The Upper Palaeolithic Age in Britain*. Oxford 1927
Garrod, D. A. E. and Bate, D. *The Stone Age of Mount Carmel*. Oxford 1937
Golomshtok, E. A. *The Old Stone Age in European Russia*. (Trans. Am. Phil. Soc. XXIX). Philadelphia 1938

Klima, B. *Dolni Vestonici.* Prague 1963
Lartet, E. and Christy, H. *Reliquiae Aquitanicae.* 1865–1875
Leakey, L. S. B. *Olduvai Gorge.* Cambridge 1951
Leakey, L. S. B. and others. *Olduvai Gorge 1951–1961,* Vol I–II. Cambridge 1965
McBurney, C. B. M. *Haua Fteah.* Cambridge In Press 1967
McBurney, C. B. M. *The Stone Age of Northern Africa.* 1960
McBurney and Hey, R. W. *Prehistory and Pleistocene Geology in Cyrenaican Libya.* 1955
Mitchell, S. R. *Stone Age Craftsmen.* Melbourne 1949
Movius, H. L. *The Lower Paleolithic Cultures of Southern and Eastern Asia* (Trans. Am. Phil. Soc. XXXIII). Philadelphia 1949
Movius, H. L. *The Irish Stone Age.* Cambridge 1942
Oakley, K. P. *Man the Toolmaker.* British Museum (Natural History) 3rd Edn. 1956
Pericot, Garcia L. *La Cueva del Parpallo.* Madrid 1942
Rust, A. *Das altsteinzeitliche Funde Von Stellmoor.* Neumunster 1937
Rust, A. *Die Alt-Und Mittle Steinzeitliche Rentierzagerlager Meiendorf.* Neumunster 1943
Rust, A. *Die Hohlenfunde von Jabrud.* Neumunster 1950
Rust, A. *Die Jungpaleolithischen Zeltenlagen von Ahrensburg.* Neumunster 1958
Schwabedissen, H. *Die Federmesser-Gruppen des Nordwest Europaischen Flachlandes.* Neumunster 1954
Smith, R. A. *Stone Age Guide.* British Museum 3rd Edn. 1926
Smith, R. A. *The Sturge Collection, Britain.* British Museum 1931
Smith, R. A. *The Sturge Collection, Foreign.* British Museum 1937
Smith, Worthington G. *Man the Primeval Savage.* London 1894
Sonneville, Bordes D. de. *Le Paléolithique Supérior en Perigord.* Bordeaux 1960
Terra, H. de and Patterson, T. T. *Studies in the Ice Age in India and Associated Human Cultures.* (Carnegie Inst. Washington) 1939
Vertes, L. *Tata (Archaeologica Hungarica N.S. XLIII).* Budapest 1964
West, R. G. *Pleistocene Geology and Biology.* London 1968

PLATES

The material of the implements is flint unless otherwise noted

PLATE I. PEBBLE TOOLS AND HAND-AXES
(Scale 1/3)

1. Quartz spheroid from Olduvai Gorge, Tanzania.
2. Basalt pebble chopping tool from Olduvai Gorge, Tanzania.
3. Quartzite pebble chopper from Kota Tampan, Malaysia.
4. Quartzite pebble chopping tool from Sauk-el-Arba, Morocco.
5 & 6. Flint chopping tools from Clacton on Sea, Essex.
7. Chopper from the Konbyinmyint terrace, Thittabwe, Burma. Thickness about half the maximum width. It is flaked on both faces, the reverse side approximately resembling the one illustrated.
8. Pointed hand-axe of primitive type from deep gravels at Fordwich, Kent. Note the poorly controlled flaking and the resulting zig-zag edge.
9. Pointed hand-axe of Middle-Acheulean *ficron* type from a working floor at Round Green, Luton, Bedfordshire.
10. Middle-Acheulean pointed hand-axe from Milton Street pit, Swanscombe, Kent.
11. Twisted ovate from the valley of the Axe, Broom, Devon.
12. Almond-shaped ovate from Milton Street pit, Swanscombe, Kent.

The profiles of Nos. 10 and 11 suggest that they were made from large flakes.

PLATE I

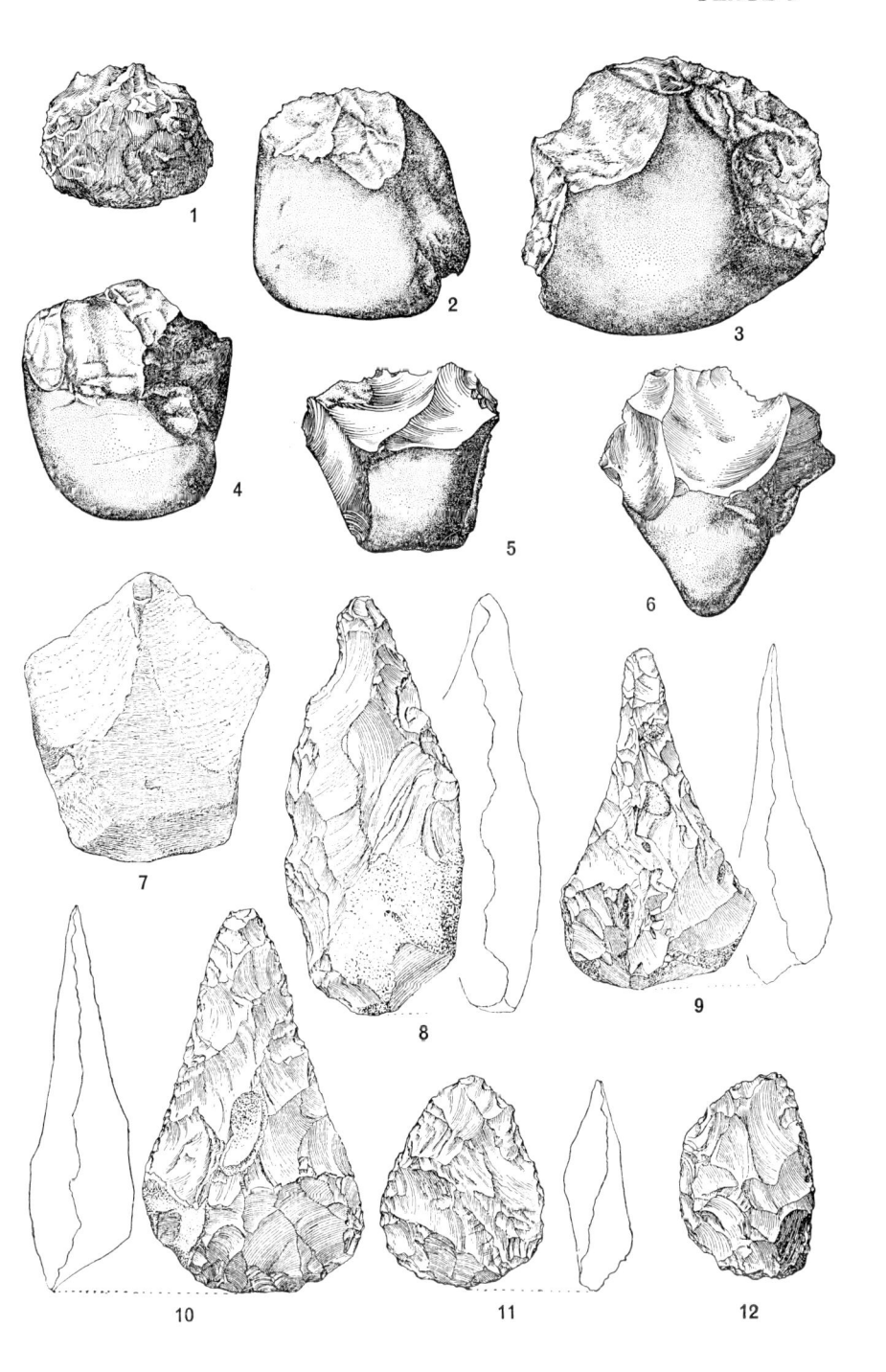

PLATE II. LATE HAND-AXES AND EARLY FLAKES
(*Scale* 1/3)

1. Cleaver from Oldoway, Tanganyika Territory. Igneous rock.
2. Cleaver from the Bournemouth district, Hampshire. Here the cleaver-edge was obtained by the final removal of an oblique flake, whereas in 1 the cleaver-edge is the original surface of the rock fragment.
3. Acheulean pointed hand-axe of late *Micoquian* type, from Yiewsley, Middlesex.
4. Late Acheulean cordate hand-axe in highly finished technique, from Bournemouth, Hampshire.
5. Cordiform hand-axe from the Mousterian working floor at Baker's Hole, Northfleet, Kent.
6. Hand-axe of the type found in the Mousterian culture, from the type-site, Le Moustier, Dordogne, France.
7—9. Clactonian flakes from basal gravels of the 100-foot terrace of the Thames at Rixon's pit, Swanscombe, Kent.
10. Clactonian flake resembling a pointed hand-axe, from the base of 100-foot gravels at Barnfield pit, Swanscombe, Kent.
11 & 12. Clactonian flakes from the type-site at Jaywick, near Clacton, Essex.
13. Highly finished tool made on Clactonian-type flake, from High Lodge Hill, Suffolk.
14 & 15. Acheulean flakes struck in the manufacture of hand-axes, from Rixon's pit (No. 14) and Barnfield pit, Swanscombe, Kent. The scars on the backs of the flakes resemble the characteristic trimming of Acheulean hand-axes.

PLATE II

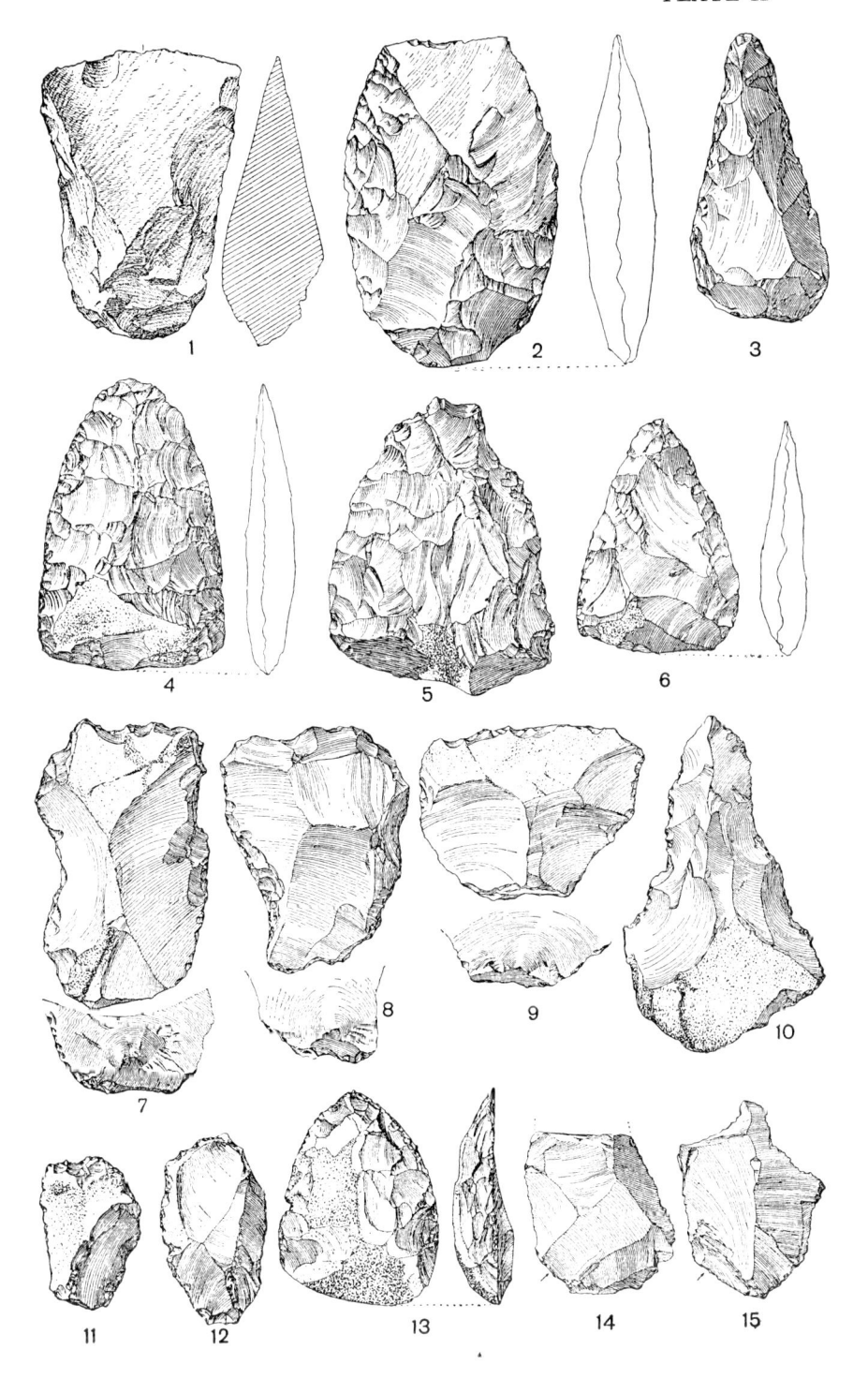

PLATE III. THE PREPARED-PLATFORM FLAKE TECHNIQUE
(*Scale* 1/3)

The reverse of all the flake tools illustrated is the main flake surface without retouch.

1. Struck tortoise core. Found with the industry underlying coombe rock at Baker's Hole, Northfleet, Kent. The shape of the main flake removed is clearly visible.

2. Untrimmed flake tool from the prepared core, from Baker's Hole, Northfleet, Kent.

3. Flake tool carefully shaped by edge-trimming after removal from the prepared core, from Baker's Hole, Northfleet, Kent.

4. Flake tool from Northern Rhodesia. The straight-edged outline was obtained by symmetrical preparation of the core, as shown by the ridges on the back of the implement.

5 & 6. Flake and point of the Levalloisian type from brick-earth at Creffield Road, Acton. The shape of the implement, No. 6, was determined by the core-preparation.

7. 'Levallois Point'. Flake point of advanced Levalloisian type from brick-earth at Crayford, Kent. This exemplifies the highest level of skill in core-preparation.

PLATE III

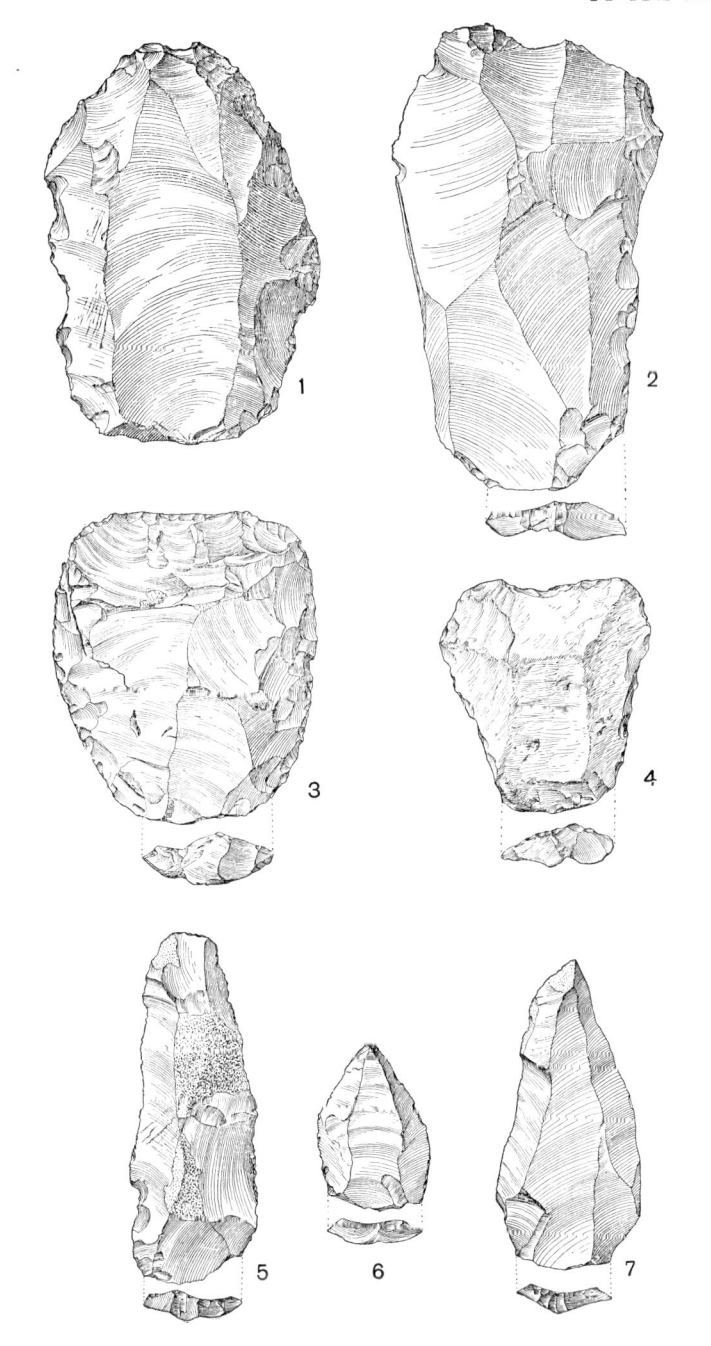

PLATE IV. LEAF-SHAPED KNIVES AND POINTS
(*Scale slightly over* 1/2)

As well as hand-axes *thin* bifacially trimmed knives and points are known from the Lower and Middle Paleolithic. The specimens in this plate belong to the Middle Paleolithic Industrial tradition.
Similar points are known in the Upper Paleolithic (pl. VI, 1 and pl. VII, 6) in France and Eastern Europe and Russia and the Neolithic (pl. VII, 23).

1. Leaf-shaped biface from La Széléta, Hungary.
   Szélétian Culture (Upper Paleolithic).
2. Leaf-shaped biface from Tit Melil, Morocco.
   Aterian Culture.
3. Leaf-shaped biface from Isenhohle, Germany.
   Mousterian Culture.
4. Leaf-shaped point from Vailly, Aisne, France.
   Mousterian or Upper Acheulian Culture.
5. Elongated leaf-shaped biface from Tit Melil, Morocco.
   Aterian Culture.
6. Leaf-shaped point, partly trimmed, from Pech de L'Azé, layer 4, Dordogne, France.
   Culture: 'Mousterian of Acheulian Tradition'.
7. Leaf-shaped biface from Laussel, Dordogne, France.
   Culture: 'Mousterian of Acheulian Tradition'.
8. 'Limace' knife with biface trimming from La Ferrassie, Layer C in the Dordogne, France.
   Culture: Ferrassie Type Mousterian.

The plate is reproduced with permission from Professor Bordes' Monograph *Typologie du Paléolithique Ancien et Moyen*, 1961.

PLATE IV

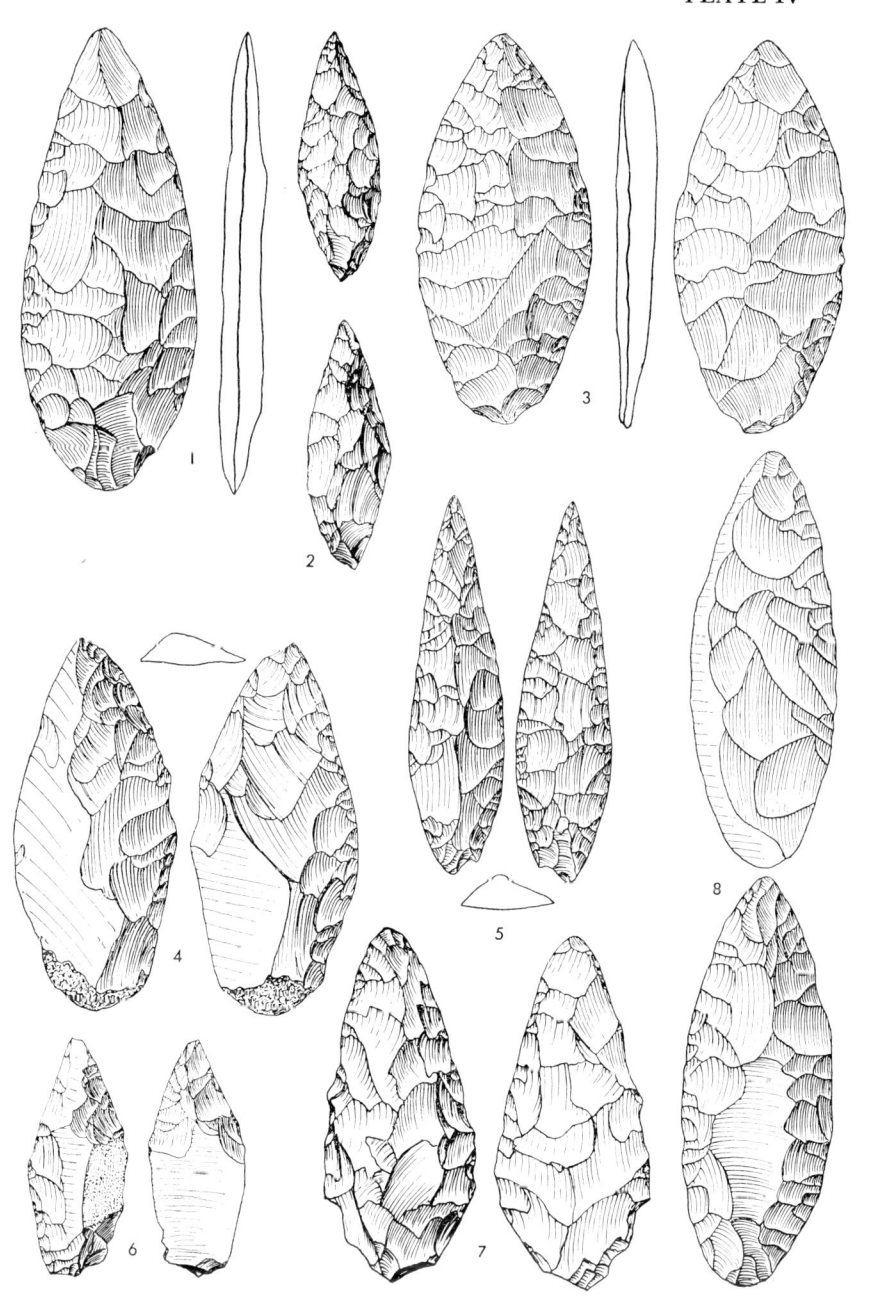

PLATE V. KNIVES, DAGGERS AND SICKLES
(*Scale* 1/3)

1. Middle Acheulean knife or scraper from the Middle Gravels, Barnfield pit, Swanscombe, Kent. This is clearly only a hand-axe with one edge left blunt.

2 & 3. Flake knives or scraper from High Lodge Hill, near Mildenhall, Suffolk. Worked on flakes of Clactonian type.

4. A carefully struck Levallois flake probably used as a knife, from Iver, Buckinghamshire.

5. Knife-chopper from Le Moustier cave, Dordogne, France, the type-site of the Mousterian culture.

6. Knife or scraper worked on a pebble selected for its grip, from Le Moustier, Dordogne.

7. Flake knife from Le Moustier, Dordogne.

8 & 9. Knives worked on flint blades from the cave of Châtelperron, Allier, France, the type-site of the Châtelperronian culture.

10 & 11. Blunted-back knives of the Gravettian culture from the cave of Les Roches, Dordogne.

12. Blunt-back knife from the Magdalenian site at Bruniquel, Tarn-et-Garonne.

13. Slug knife of the Food Vessel culture from Castle Carrock, Cumberland.

14. Neolithic sickle in highly finished technique from Egypt. The reverse side is left smooth save for a narrow band of flake-scars around the outside. The inset of the reverse side (magnified to twice the scale of the main drawing) shows the extremely fine serration of the edge.

15. Neolithic sickle found near Eastbourne, Sussex.

16. Discoidal knife with polished edge, perhaps of the Beaker (Early Bronze Age) period, from Arbor Low Stone Circle, Derbyshire.

17. Dagger of type associated with the 'A' division of the Beaker culture, from Bottisham Lode, Cambridgeshire.

18. Dagger of the late Neolithic period in Denmark. The shape has been influenced by contemporary metal types imported from the south.

PLATE V

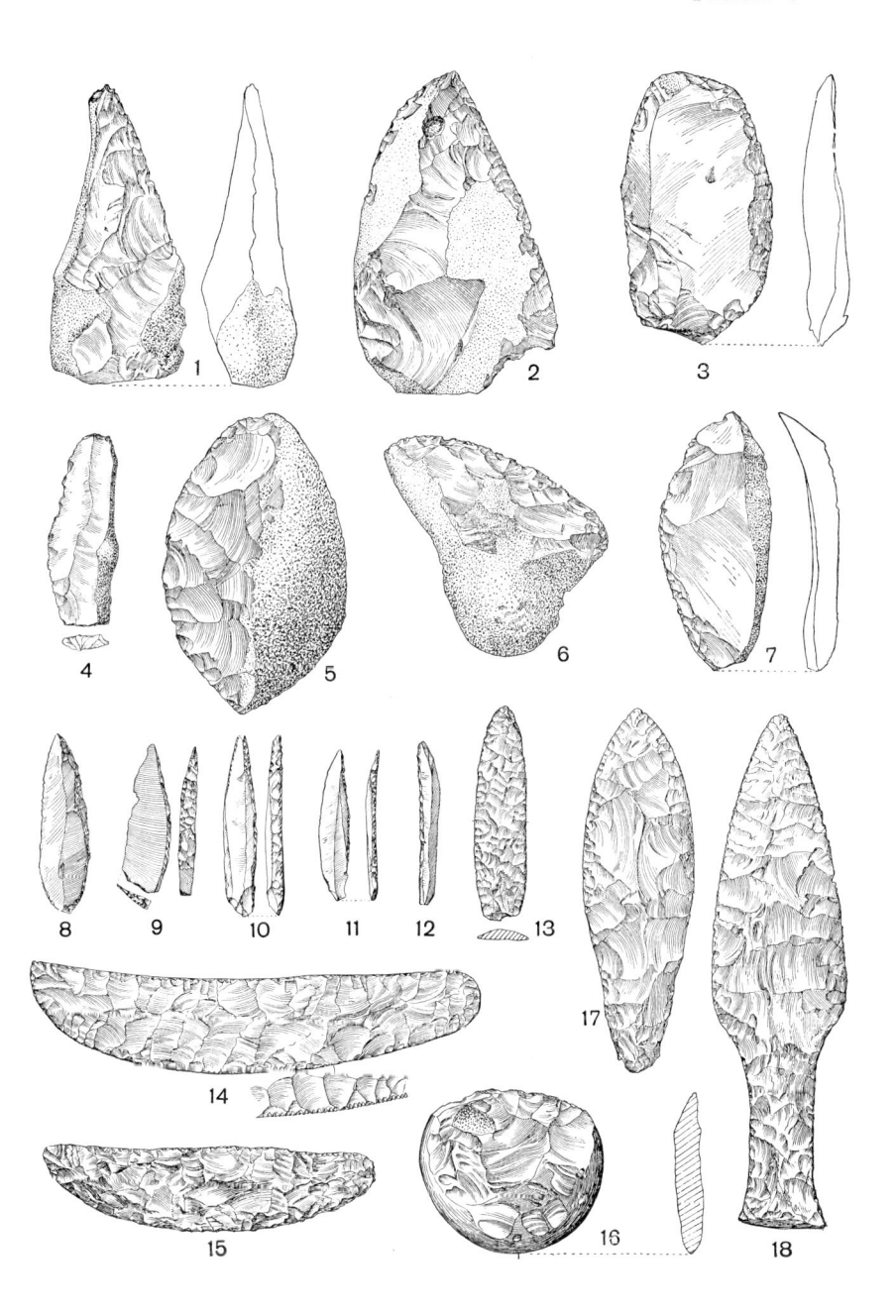

PLATE VI. SCRAPERS

(*Scale slightly under* 1/2)

1. Clactonian scraper from the basal gravel of the Hoxnian aggradation at Rixon's pit, Swanscombe, Kent.
2. Acheulean side-scraper from Sturry, Kent.
3. Mousterian side-scraper from Le Moustier, Dordogne.
4. Side-scraper of the industry at High Lodge, near Mildenhall, Suffolk. The piece is very thick, the cross-section coming near to an equilateral triangle.
5. A more carefully shaped side-scraper from High Lodge (see No. 4).
6. End-scraper from High Lodge (see No. 4).
7. Aurignacian end-scraper on a thick blade, from Laugerie Haute, Les Eyzies, Dordogne.

8 & 9. End-scrapers on blades, probably Aurignacian, respectively from Laugerie Haute, Dordogne, and Gorge d'Enfer, Les Eyzies, Dordogne. The two parallel ridges along the back of blade No. 9 are deliberate and a typical feature.

10. Nosed scraper of the Aurignacian culture from Belcaire Bas, St. Léon-sur-Vézère, Dordogne.
11. Scraper ('raclette') of the Early Magdalenian culture, on a thin flake with a very steeply trimmed edge, from Laugerie Haute, Dordogne.
12. End-scraper of the Mesolithic Forest culture, from Lower Halstow, Kent.
13. Mesolithic end-scraper from Kelling Heath, Norfolk.

14 & 15. Scrapers of the Neolithic Windmill Hill culture, from the type-site in Wiltshire.

16—19. Scrapers found on the surface of fields near Icklingham, Suffolk. No. 16 may be Neolithic, the remainder more probably of the Bronze Age, of which the carefully worked No. 19 is typical. No. 17 is peculiar in being trimmed by pressure from the upper side of the flake (inverse retouch), the top of the scraper shown in the figure being formed of the main flake surface.

PLATE VI

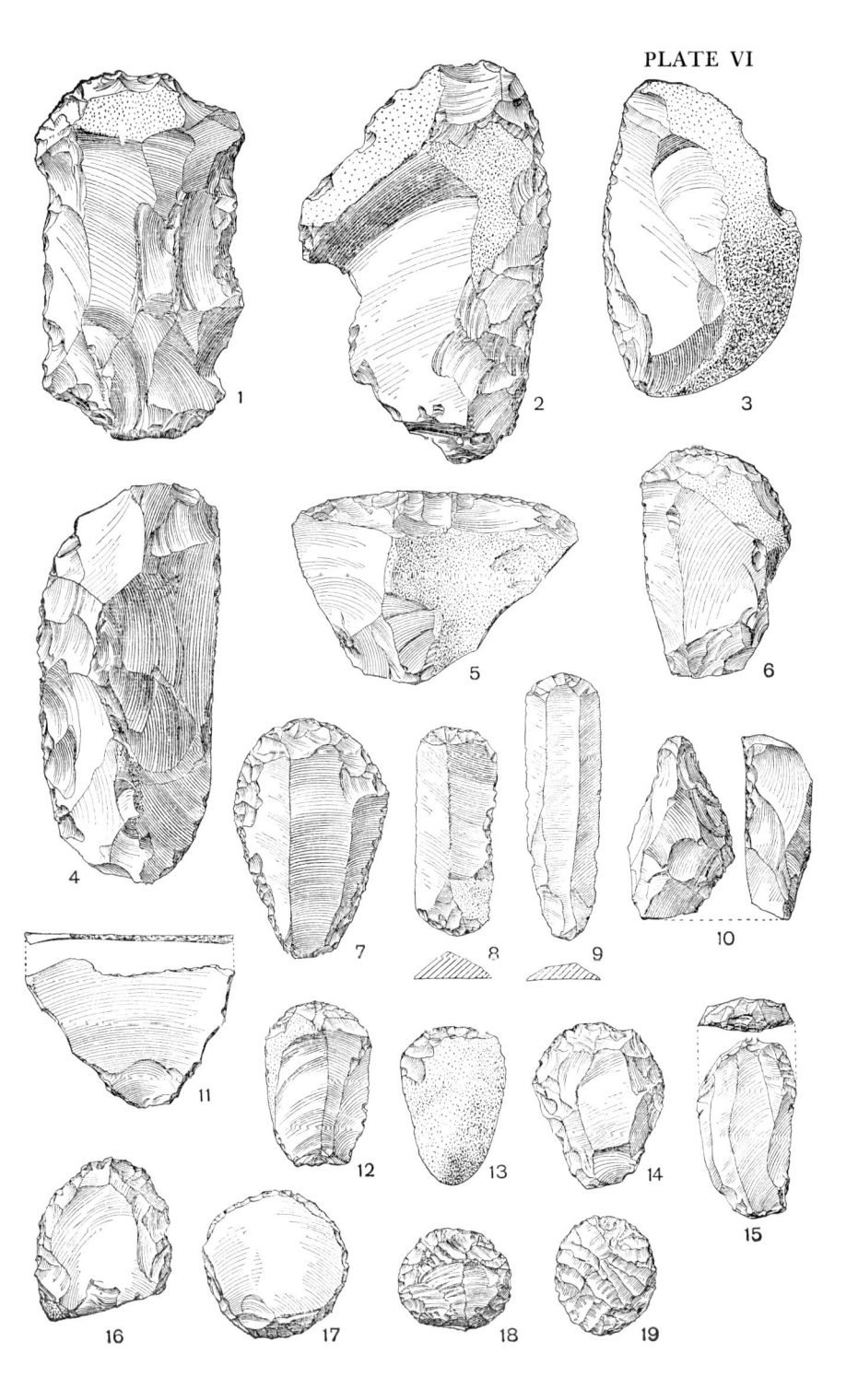

PLATE VII. ARROWHEADS AND OTHER PROJEC-
TILE POINTS
(*Scale* 1/2)

1. The earliest form of tanged point, of the Aterian culture, found at Ras 'Amar, Cyrenaica.
2—5. Single-shouldered and tanged ('Font-Robert') points of the Gravettian (Nos. 2, 3) and the Solutrean (Nos. 4, 5) cultures. No. 5 is worked on a laurel-leaf point resembling No. 6 (2 from Grotte de l'Eglise, 3 from Laugerie Basse, 4 from Les Roches, 5 from Laugerie Haute).
6. Willow-leaf point, worked on both faces, of the Solutrean culture, from the type-site at Solutré.
7. A Solutrean tanged-and-barbed arrowhead from the Cave of Parpalló, Valencia, Spain. This Solutrean type, which is not so far known outside Spain, is separated by many thousands of years from the closely similar Bronze-Age arrowheads such as Nos. 21 and 22.
8—11. Transverse arrowheads of Mesolithic or Neolithic date. No. 8 is from Denmark, Nos. 9—11 from Derbyshire. The last three show clearly the transmutation of the original type.
12—14. Bifacially worked leaf-shaped points of Neolithic date, from County Antrim; Northdale, Yorkshire, and Mildenhall, respectively.
15 & 16. Hollow-base and tanged points from the Kawar, near Bilma, Southern Sahara, typical of the 'Sahara Neolithic' industries.
17 & 18. Hollow-base and tanged points from the Fayum lake-basin, Egypt. The meticulous workmanship is typical of the Egyptian flint craft of the Neolithic and the earlier part of the Bronze Age.
19. Hollow base arrowhead with short barbs from Northern Ireland.
20—22. Tanged and tanged-and-barbed arrowheads of the British late Neolithic. No. 20 from Charlbury, Oxfordshire; No. 21 from Stonesfield, Oxfordshire; No. 22 from the neighbourhood of Cambridge, Early Bronze Age.
23. Neolithic laurel leaf from the Mildenhall area.
24 & 25. 'Bann' points from Co. Down, Ireland, probably of Neolithic date but representing a Mesolithic flint tradition.
26. Late Neolithic arrowhead with a triangular cross section and tapered tang, from Denmark.
27. Bronze Age tanged arrowhead from Ireland, No. 24 from Ballymena, Antrim, No. 25 unlocated in Northern Ireland.

PLATE VII

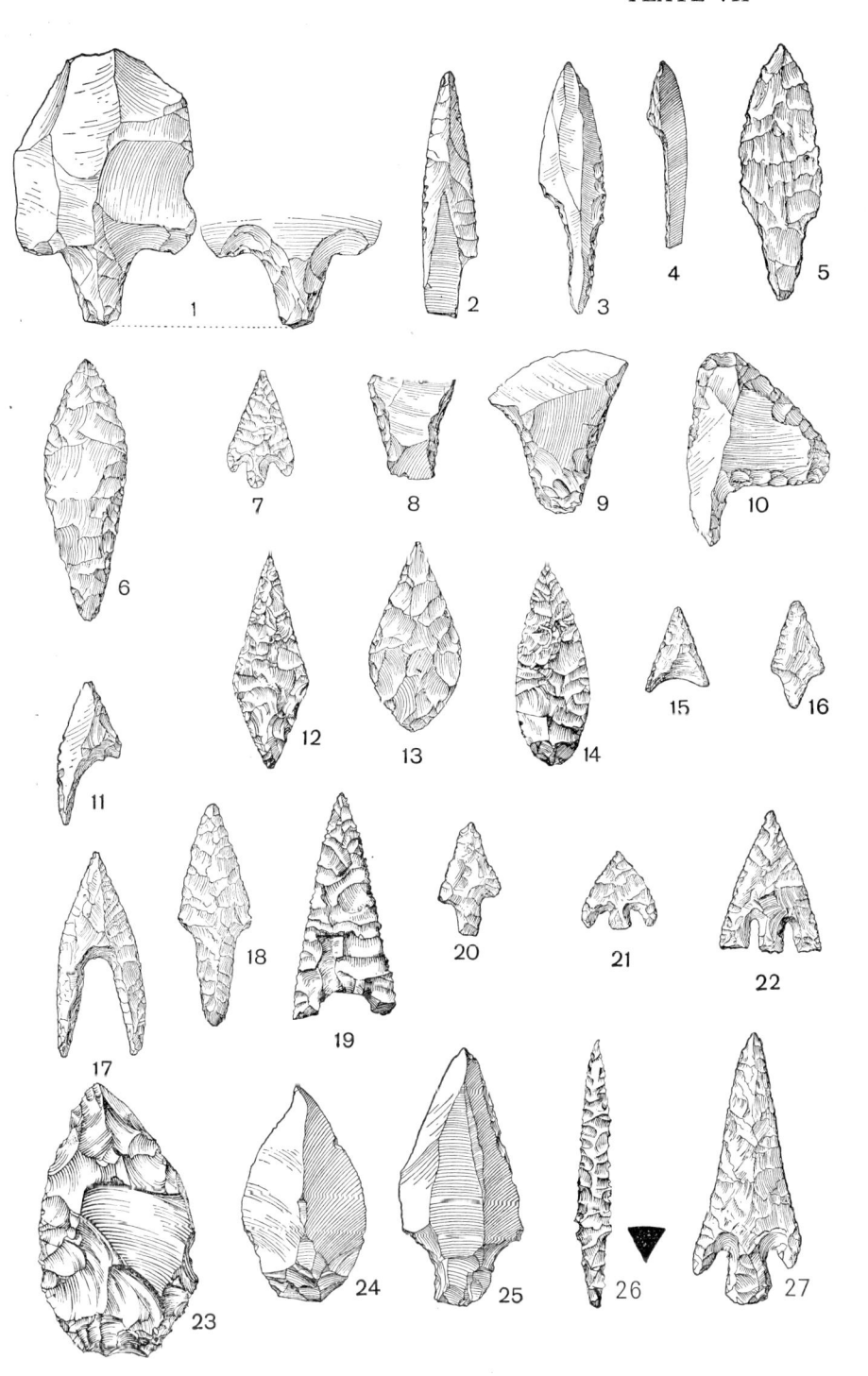

PLATE VIII. BURINS AND MICROLITHS
(Scale 1/3)

The chisel or gouge-disc working edge of the burin is formed by removing small flakes from the point of the tool, on the thin edge of the flake. The small arrows show the direction of the blow or blows struck to produce the 'burin facet'.

1—4. 'Angle' burins, in which a burin facet meets an edge trimmed by chipping. 1 from Les Roches; 2 and 4 from Laugerie Haute, Les Eyzies, Dordogne; 3 from Limeuil, Dordogne.

5—8. Burins with opposed burin facets. The simplest form, 5 and 7, with single opposed facets, is called a bec-de-flûte; those with more facets polyhedral. No. 8 has a burin edge at both ends; 5 from St Geniès, Dordogne; 6 from Gorge d'Enfer, Les Eyzies, Dordogne; 7 from Tremolat, Dordogne; 8 from Dordogne.

9. A burin busqué, or convex burin, akin to a nosed scraper, made on a thick blade often of triangular section. The rounded nose is formed by the meeting of several small facets with a single flake surface. There is usually a blunted notch near the nose. From La Balutie, Dordogne.

10 & 11. 'Parrot-beak' burins from La Madeleine, Dordogne, type-site of the Magdalenian culture.

12. Borer of the Mesolithic Forest culture, from Lower Halstow, Kent.

13 & 14. Rough blades with partially blunted back, mesolithic type, from Kelling Heath, Norfolk.

(Scale 2/3)

15. Magdalenian borer for piercing the eyes of needles, from Bruniquel, Tarn-et-Garonne.

16. Microlithic blunted-back blade from Bruniquel, Tarn-et-Garonne.

17—33. Microliths of geometric type: 17—20, 26, 27, 29, 31 from Lakenheath, Suffolk; 21, 22 from Capwith Hill, Lancashire; 23, 24 from March Hill, Yorkshire; 25, 32 from Manton Warren, Lincolnshire; 28 from Warcote Hill, Yorkshire; 33 from Kelling Heath, Norfolk.

34—39. Microliths of non-geometric type: 30 from Trevose Head, Cornwall; 34, 35, 38 from Kelling Heath, Norfolk; 36 and 37 from Scunthorpe, Lincolnshire; 39 from Lower Halstow, Kent.

40—48. Geometric microliths from a surface site at Foughala, near Tolga, Sud Constantinois, North Africa.

PLATE VIII

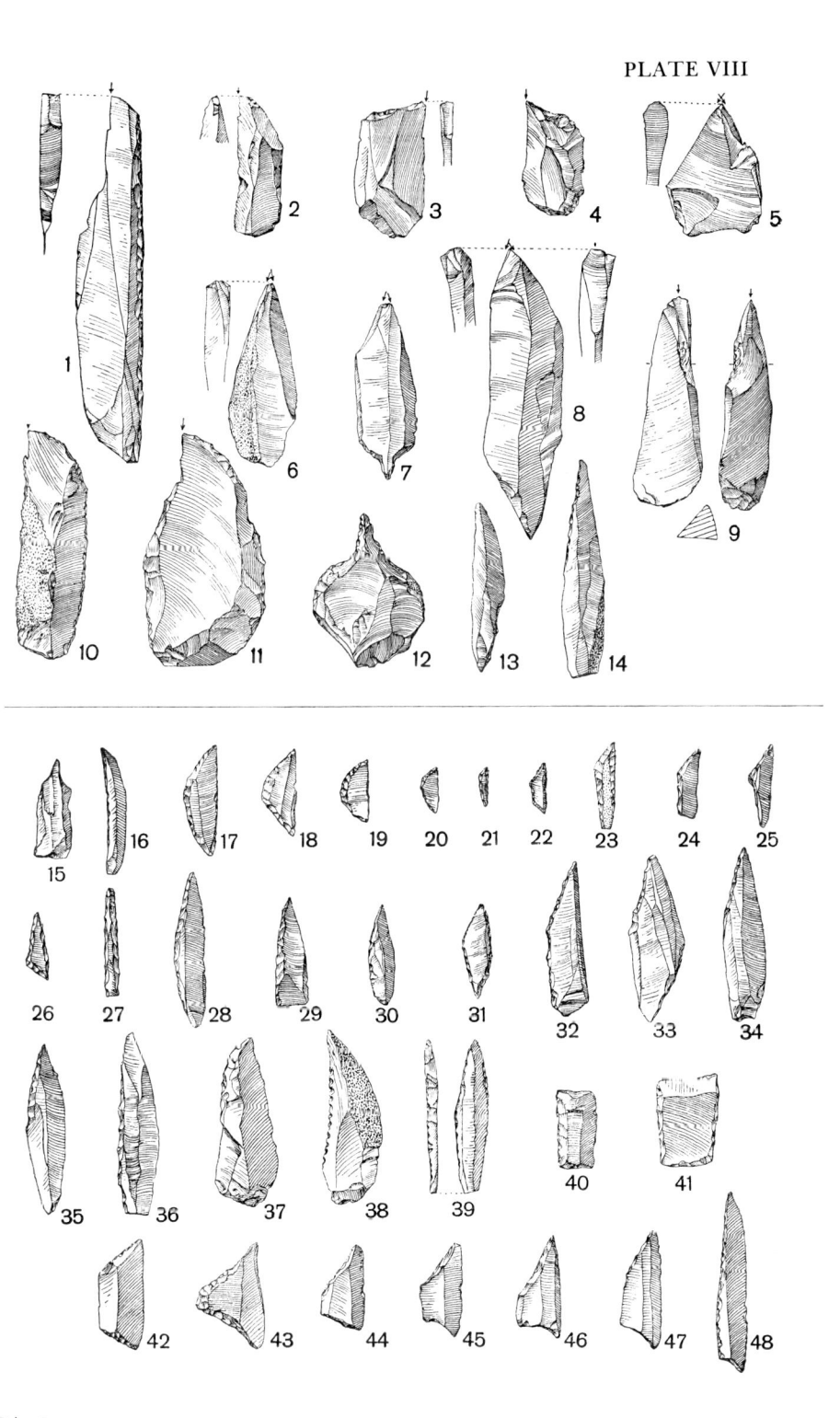

PLATE IX. AXE-HEADS USED FOR TREE FELLING
(*Scale* 1/3)

1. Flake axe from a Mesolithic site at Lower Halstow, Kent.
2. A 'Thames pick' from Farnham, Surrey. The cutting-edge on this and the preceding axe was obtained by removing a single transverse flake ('tranchet' technique): see No. 3.
3. Sharpening flake struck off a Mesolithic axe, from Kelling Heath, Norfolk.
4—6. Neolithic axes from Great Bealing, Suffolk; Easton Down, Wiltshire; and Bexley Heath, Kent.
7 & 8. Neolithic axes with splayed blades, possibly influenced by metal forms, from Bottisham Fen, Cambridge, and the Thames at Teddington.
9—11. Neolithic polished axes, 9 and 10 from the Thames at Teddington and Mildenhall, Suffolk; 11 (sandstone) from Hunstow, E. R., Yorkshire.
12. Polished greenstone axe, probably of the Early Bronze Age, from Merton, Cambridgeshire.

PLATE IX

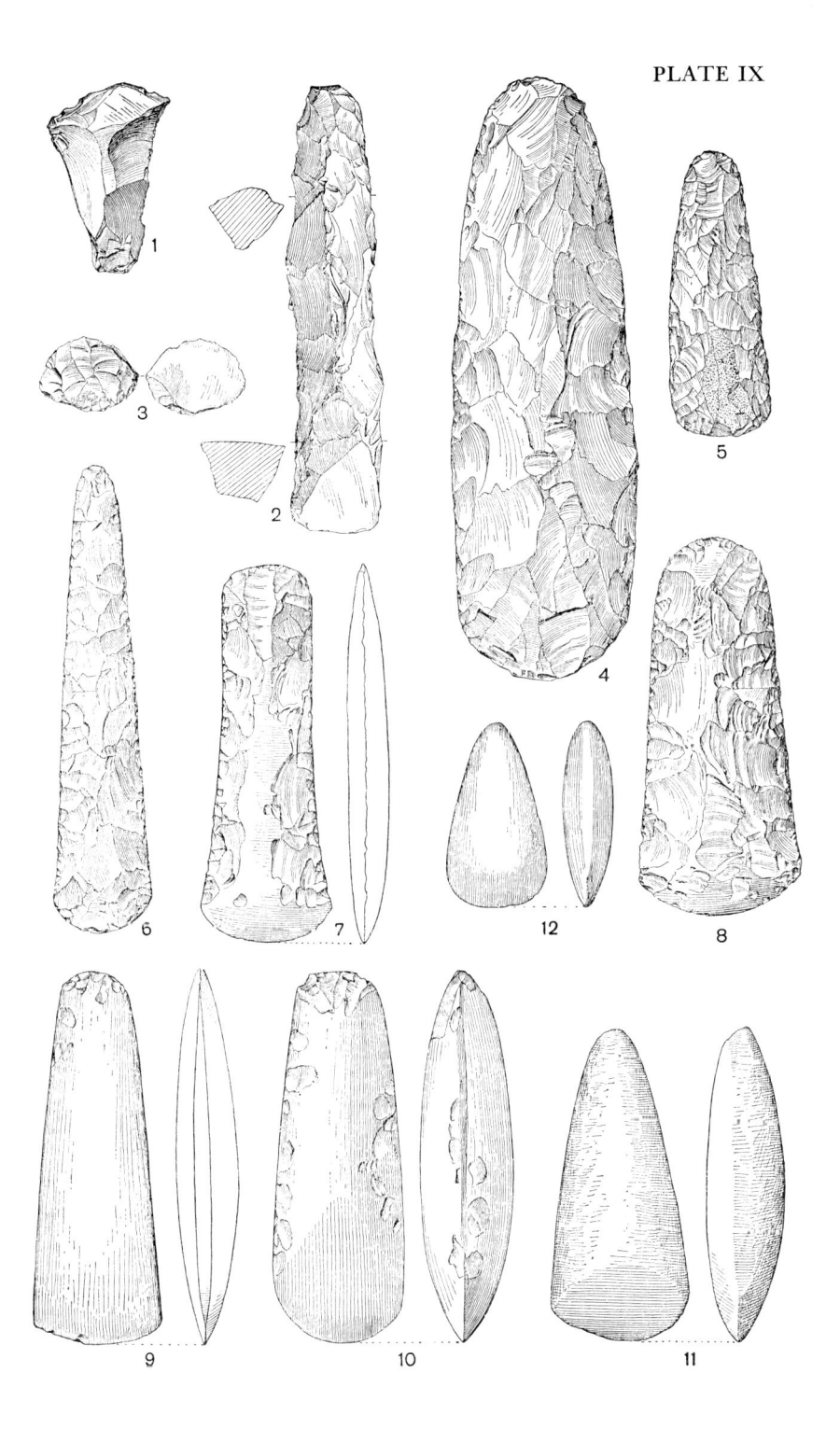

PLATE X. PERFORATED STONE AXES, MACE-HEADS AND ANTLER MOUNTING

(*Scale* 1/3)

1. Axe of the type associated on rare occasions with the Beaker People, found at Kingston-on-Thames.

2. Battle-axe of the Early Bronze Age of Camerton Snowshill type, found at Battersea, London.

3. Mace-head probably of the Early Bronze Age, found in Threadneedle Street, London.

4. Battle-axe of Early Bronze Age type, found at Toft Monks, Norfolk.

5. Battle-axe from Sweden, late Neolithic or Early Bronze Age.

6. Neolithic axe in antler sleeve shaped for mounting in haft, from Wangen, Switzerland.

7. Mace-head from Marlborough, Wiltshire, of Mesolithic date.

PLATE X

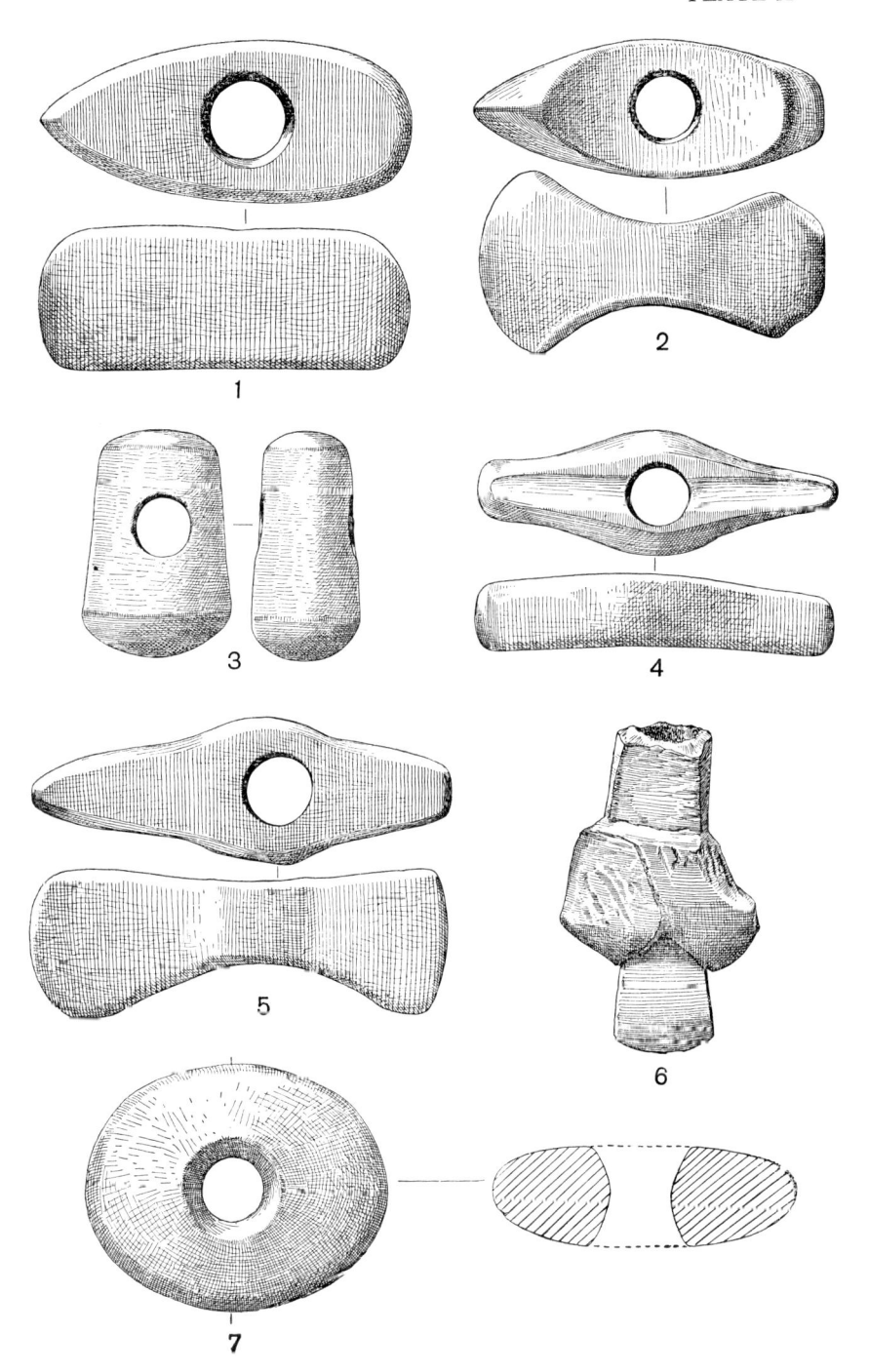

1

2

3

4

5

6

7

PLATE XI. SICKLE BLADES
(*Scale* 1/1)

1. Short blade segment with finely serrated edge, from Mildenhall.

2. Blade knife or sickle, sharpened by grinding and polishing along one edge. Probably from a Late Neolithic barrow near Biggin in Derbyshire.

3. Bifacially worked sickle blade with a short tang for hafting, and with a straight cutting edge. Late Neolithic or Beaker Age, from the Mildenhall area.

4. Bifacially worked sickle blade with a curved concave cutting edge. Late Neolithic, from Denmark.

PLATE XI

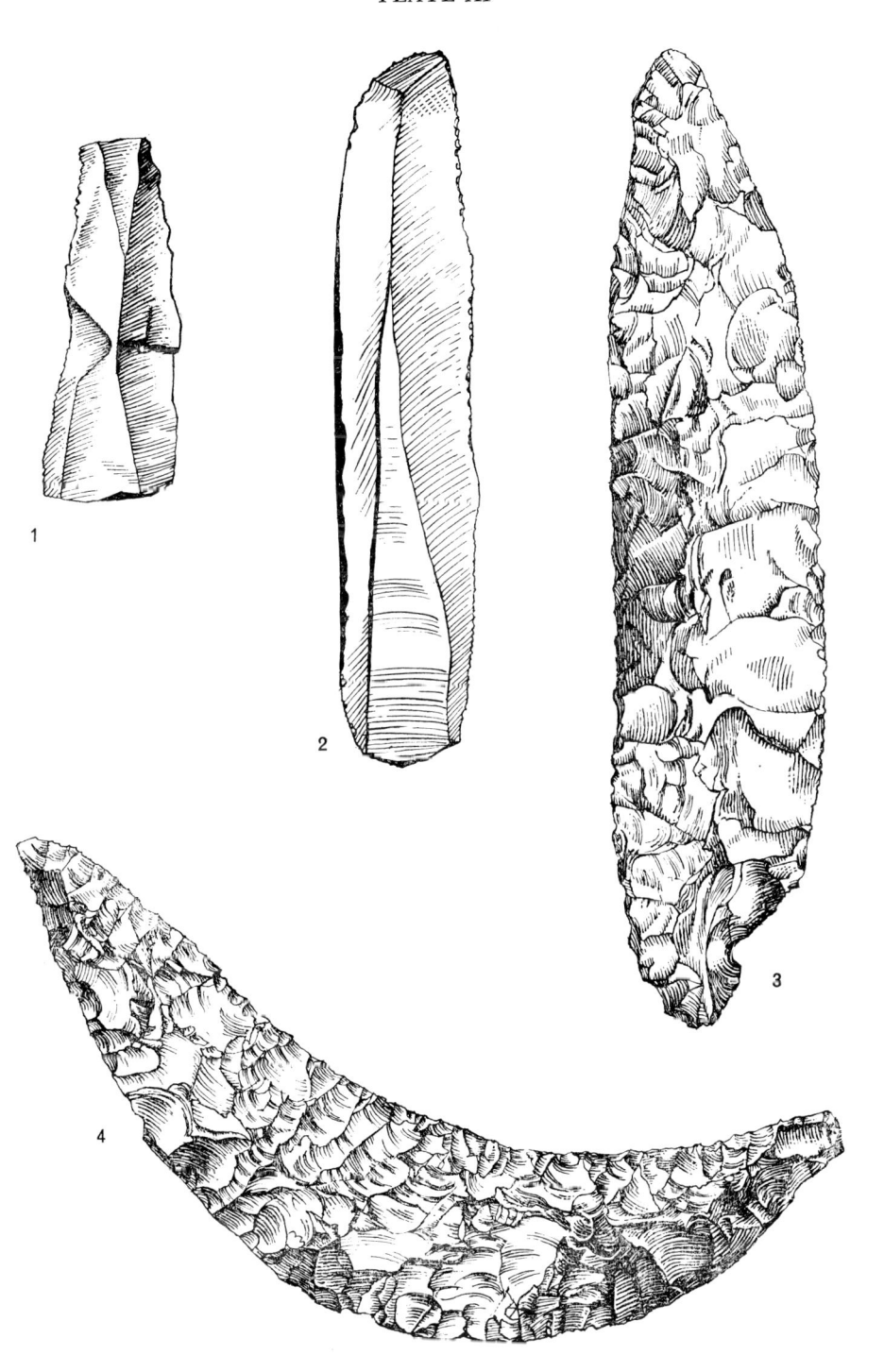

INDEX

Abbeville, France 45, 46, 49
Abrasion 35
Acheulean culture 38, 45–53, 56
Africa 13, 19, 20, 23, 39, 41, 46, 57, 61
Altamira, Spain 68
America 11, 35
Animals 10*n*, 20, 58, 66, 70, 72, 74
Antler 24, 68, 70, 72
Antrim, County, Ireland Pl. VII
Anyathian 45*n*
Arbor Low Stone Circle, Derbyshire Pl. V
Argon *See* Potassium Argon
Arrowheads 59, 64, 67, 70, 76; Pl. VII
Art 66, 68, 69
Asia 11, 45, 57
Aterian culture 59, 67; Pls. IV, VII
Aurignacian culture 38, 64, 65, 66
Australia 37, 68*n*
Aveline's Hole, Mendips 69
Axes 71, 75, 77; Pls. IX, X

Bakers Hole, Kent 55, 56, 58
Barrows 76
Battle-axes 75, 77; Pl. X
Beaker culture 76; Pl. V
Belcaire Bas, St. Léon-sur-Vézère, Dordogne, France Pl. VI
Bexley Heath, Kent Pl. IX
Biggin, Derbyshire Pl. XI
Blade cores 61; fig. 12

Blade cultures *See* Aurignacian, Magdalenian, Gravettian, Creswellian
Blade technique 61–3; fig. 12
Blades 60, 64, 65, 67, 69, 72
Bone
  Compressors 36
  Engraving 69
  Tools 70
Borers 24, 70; Pl. VIII
Bottisham Lode, Cambridgeshire, Pls. V, IX
Boulder-clay 12
Bournemouth Hampshire Pl. II
Bow 59, 67
Bronze Age 77
Broom, Devon 82; Pl. I
Broxbourne, Hertfordshire 71
Bruniquel, Tarn-et-Garonne, France Pls. V, VIII
Bull-head bed 26
Bulbs of percussion 28, 30, 44, 47
Burins 60, 63, 64, 66, 67, 69, 70; Pl. VIII
Burma 23, 45

Caddington, Bedfordshire 52
Cae Gwyn, Vale of Clwyd, Wales 69
Cambridge Pl. VII
Capwith Hill, Lancashire Pl. VIII
Carbon 14. *See* Radiocarbon
Castle Carrock, Cumberland Pl. V

Cave-paintings 40, 66 & *n*, 68
Caversham, Berks. 50
Ceylon 68*n*
'Chapeau de gendarme' 56
Charlbury, Oxfordshire Pl. VII
Châtelperron, Allier, France Pl. V
Châtelperronian 65; Pl. V
Chellean 45
China 17, 19, 45
Choppers 43, 45, 60; fig. 8; Pl. I
Chopping tools 43, 53; Pl. I
Choukoutien 45*n*, 58
Cissbury, Sussex 76
Clacton-on-Sea, Essex 44; Pl. I
Clactonian culture 38, 43–5, 58; fig. 6
Choppers 43; Pl. I
Cores 43, 53; fig. 6
Flakes 43, 44; fig. 6; Pl. II
Cleavers 51; Pl. II
Combe Grenal, Western France 60
Conchoidal fracture 28–30; fig. 2
Cones of percussion 26–7, 35; fig. 1
Coombe Rock, Northfleet, Kent 56
Core-axe 71
Cortex 25
Cotswolds 33
Crags of East Anglia 16
Crayford, Kent 56; Pl. III
Creffield Road, Acton, London 56

104

Creswell Crags, Derbyshire 69, 71
Creswellian culture 38, 69, 71
Cultures
 Acheulean 38, 45-63; Pls. I, II, V, VI
 African Acheulean 57
 Aterian 59, 67; Pls. IV, VII
 Aurignacian 38, 64, 65, 66; Pl. VI
 Clactonian 38, 43-5, 58; Pl. VI
 Creswellian 38, 69, 71
 Food vessel 77; Pl. V
 Gravettian 38, 69, 71; Pl. VIII
 Larnian 74
 Levalloisian 51, 53-7, 58; fig. 10; Pls. III, IV
 Magdalenian 38, 67-8, 68-70, 71; Pls. VI, VIII
 Maglemose 71
 Mousterian 38, 56, 58-61; figs. 8, 11; Pls. II, V, VI
 Perigordian 64, 65
 Rinyo-Clacton 77
 Sauvetarrian 72
 Solutrean 48, 59, 66-7; Pl. VII
 Szélétian Pl. IV
 Stellenbosch 51
 Tardenoisian 72
 Windmill Hill 76, 78; Pl. VI

Daggers 75, 76, 77
De Geer, Baron 21
Denmark 10, 75; Pls. VII, XI
Denticulate Mousterian 60
Derived specimens 35
Disc core 58; fig. 11

Discoidal knife 77
Don Basin 65
Down, County, Ireland Pl. VII

Eastbourne, Sussex Pl. V
Easton Down, Wiltshire Pl. IX
Egypt 20, 37
Et-Tabun, Mount Carmel, Palestine 45

Faceted butts 54, 57, 58; fig. 10; Pl. III; *see also* Levalloisian technique
Farming cultures 74-6
Farnham, Surrey Pl. IX
Fayum lake-basin, Egypt Pl. VII
Fens, The 33
Ferrasie Mousterian 60
Ffynnon Beuno, Vale of Clwyd, Wales 69
Figurines 66
Fingnoan 45*n*
Finland 21
Flakes 43, 58, 66, 77
 African Acheulean 57
 Acheulean 51, 52; Pl. II
 Clactonian 43, 44; Pls. II, IV
 Levalloisian 51, 53; Pls. III, IV
Flandrian or post-glacial period 10*n*
Font de Gaume 68
Font Robert points 65, 67; Pl. VII
Food vessel culture 77; Pl. V
Fordwich, Kent Pl. I
Fossils 20
Foughala, near Tolga, Constantinois, N. Africa Pl. VIII

Fracture, types of
 Conchoidal 28, 29, 30; fig. 2
 Hinge 29-30, 49; fig. 3
 Mechanical 26-9; fig. 1
 Pot-lid 31; fig. 4
 Starch (columnar) 32; fig. 5
 Thermal 30-1
Frost-pitting 31; fig. 4

Gaddesden Row, Hertfordshire 51
Germany 11, 21
Glaciations 11-12, 13, 16
 Elster 11, 20, 43
 Säale 11, 53, 56
 Weichsel 11, 56
Gloss 35
Graig Lwyd rock 24
Grand Pressigny, Le 24
Gravettian culture 38, 59, 64, 65, 66, 67; Pls. V, VII
Great Bealing, Suffolk Pl. IX
Great Langdale, Cumberland 76
Grimes Graves, Norfolk 76

Hamburgian culture 69
Hammer-stones 36
Hand-axes 46-53, 58; figs. 7, 9
 Abbevillean 46, 49; Pl. I
 Acheulean 46, 48, 50, 51, 52, 60; Pls. I, II
 Cordate 51; Pl. II
 Levallois Pl. III
 Manufacture 47-9
 Mousterian Pl. II
 Ovates 46, 47, 51
 Pointed 46, 47, 51; fig. 9; Pl. I
Harpoons 24, 63, 69, 71

Holocene or Recent period 20
Homo neanderthalensis 60, 61
Homo sapiens 43, 61
Hoxne, Suffolk 9, 16
Hungary 43, 67
Hunstow, East Riding of Yorkshire Pl. IX

Icklingham, Suffolk Pl. VI
India 45, 46, 57, 58, 68n
Interglacials 11, 16
 Cromerian 11, 20, 46, 49
 Hoxnian 11, 43, 47, 50
 Eemian 11, 20, 51, 56, 57
Inverse retouch 90
'Iron-mould' 34
Isenhohle, Germany Pl. IV
Iver, Buckinghamshire Pl. V

Java 19, 45
Jaywick, Essex Pl. II

Kawar, near Bilma, Southern Sahara Pl. VII
Kelling Heath, Norfolk Pls. VI, VIII, IX
Kent's Cavern, Torquay, Devon 61, 68
Kenya 23
Kingston-on-Thames Pl. X
Knives 63, 64, 77; Pl. V
Konbyinmyint terrace, Thittabwe, Burma Pl. I
Kota Tampan, Malaysia Pl. 82

La Balutie, Dordogne, France Pl. VIII

La Ferrassie, Dordogne, France Pl. IV
La Garenne, Dordogne, France 18
La Madeleine, Dordogne, France Pl. VIII
La Micoque, France 45
La Széléta, Hungary Pl. IV
Lakenheath, Suffolk Pl. VIII
Larnian culture 74
Lascaux, Dordogne, France 18
Laugerie Haute, Les Eyzies, Dordogne, France Pls. VI, VIII
Laussel, Dordogne, France Pl. IV
Leaf-shaped knives and points 59, 66, 67, 76, 77 Pls. IV, VII
Le Martinet, Sauveterre-le-Lemance, France 72
Le Moustier, Dordogne, France Pls. II, V, VI
Les Eyzies, Dordogne, France Pls. VI, VIII
Les Roches, Dordogne, France Pls. V, VIII
Levalloisian technique 51, 53–7, 58; fig. 10
Limeuil, Dordogne, France Pl. VIII
Loess 16–17 & n
London
 Battersea Pl. X
 Grays Inn Lane, Black Mary's 9
 Threadneedle Street Pl. X
Lower Halstow, Kent Pls. VI, VIII, IX
Luton (Round Green), Bedfordshire Pl. I

Mace-head 78; Pl. X
Magdalenian culture 38, 67–8, 69–70, 71
Maglemose culture 71
Main Coombe Rock 15–16
Main flake surface 28
Malaya 45
Manton Warren, Lincolnshire Pl. VIII
March Hill, Yorkshire Pl. VIII
Marlborough, Wiltshire Pl. X
Melos 23
Mendip caves 69
Merton, Cambridgeshire Pl. IX
Mesolithic, defined 38–9
Mesolithic of Europe 69–74
Microburin 73; fig. 13
Microliths 67–8 & n, 70, 71, 72, 73; fig. 13; Pl. VIII
Migration 17
Mildenhall, Suffolk 44; Pls. II, IV, VI, VII, IX, X
Moraines 12, 20
Morocco 43
Mother Grundy's Parlour, Creswell Crags, Derbyshire 69
Mousterian culture 38, 56, 58–61; figs. 8, 11; Pl. IV
Disc core 58; fig. 11

Needles 24
Neolithic
 Defined 39–40
 Farmers 74–6
New Zealand 37
Nile Valley 20
Northdale, Yorkshire Pl. VII
Northern Ireland Pl. VII

Northfleet, Kent Pls. II, III

Oban, Oronsay 73-4
Oldbury Hill, near Ightham, Kent 61
Oldowan culture 42
Oldoway, Tanganyika Pl. II
Olduvai Gorge, Tanzania 42; Pl. I
Olduvai range 19
Olorgesailie, Kenya 52
Ovates 46, 51; Pl. I

Palaeolithic
  Defined 37-8
  Lower Palaeolithic See Acheulean, Clactonian
  Middle Palaeolithic See Mousterian, Aterian
  Upper Palaeolithic in Europe 63
  Upper Palaeolithic in Britain 68-9
  Upper Palaeolithic See also Blade cultures
Palestine 45, 61, 65
Parpalló, Valencia, Spain 67; Pl. VII
Patination 26, 32-3, 34, 35
Patjitanian 45n
Paviland Cave, Gower Peninsula, Wales 69
Pebble tools 42, 43, 53; Pl. I
Pech de L'Azé, Dordogne, France Pl. IV
Penmaenmawr, N. Wales 24, 75
Perigordian culture 64, 65
Picks 24
Pleistocene period 9, 10 & n, 12-17, 18, 20

Points
  Antler 71-2
  Bone 2
  Flint 51, 56, 59, 65, 69
Pollen 21-2
Potassium Argon dating 19, 42
Pot-boilers 36
Pressure technique 36, 48, 66, 77

Quaternary 10n
Quina Mousterian 44, 60

Radiocarbon dating 18, 19, 76
Ras 'Amar, Cyrenaica Pl. VII
Recent period 20, 21
Resolved flaking 48
Rinyo-Clacton culture 77
Robin Hood's Cave, Creswell Crags, Derbyshire 69
Rolling 35

Sahara Neolithic Pl. VII
St. Acheul, France 45
St. Brelade, Jersey 61
St. Geniès, Dordogne, France Pl. VIII
Sauk-el-Arba, Morocco Pl. I
Sauveterrian culture 72
Scandinavia 21
Scrapers 44, 51, 60, 63, 64, 66, 67, 69, 70, 71, 76, 77; Pl. VI
Sculpture 67
Scunthorpe, Lincolnshire Pl. VIII
Sickles 76; Pls. V, XI
Slug-knife 77
Soan 45n, 58
Solifluxion 15
Solutrean culture 48, 59, 66-7; Pl. VII

Somme Valley, France 9, 17, 19
Spearheads 71
Staining of flint 33-5
Star Carr, Yorkshire 71
Stellenbosch culture 51
Step-flaking 44, 48, 59; fig. 8
Stonesfield, Oxfordshire Pl. VII
Striations 35
Striking platform 27, 44, 62
Sturry, Kent Pl. VI
Summertown terrace 14
Sussex Downs, The 33
Swanscombe, Kent 26, 50, 52; Pls. I, II, V, VI
Syria 61, 65
Szelétian culture Pl. IV

Tampanian 45n
Tanzania 42
Tardenoisian culture 72
Tayacian 44
Terminology of cultures 37-40
Terraces 12 16
Tertiary era 10
Téviec, Brittany 72
Thames pick 71; Pl. IX
Thames, River, at Teddington Pl. IX
Thames Valley 14, 15-16, 17, 19, 26, 44, 50
Tit Melil, Morocco Pl. IV
Toad-belly' patina 33, 35
Toralba, near Madrid, Spain 52
Tortoise-cores 54, 55; Pl. III
Trade 23-4, 75, 76
Transcaucasia 66
Tremolat, Dordogne, France Pl. VIII

107

Trevose Head, Cornwall
  Pl. VIII
Tundra 16
Typology 22

Vailly, Aisne, France Pl.
  IV
Vertes Zöllos, Hungary 43

Vig, Eastern Denmark 72

Wangen, Switzerland Pl.
  X
Wansunt, Lower Thames
  51
Warcote Hill, Yorkshire
  94

Warren Hill, Suffolk 33
White Hill, near Huddersfield, Yorkshire 73
Windmill Hill culture 76, 78

Yiewsley, Middlesex Pl. II

THE PLEISTOCENE

Glaciations	Cultures		
	Core	Flake	Blade

Glaciations	Core	Flake	Blade
Hunstantan Glaciation			Creswellian Magdalenian Solutrean Gravettian Aurignacian Châtel- perronian
Eemian Interglacial		Mousterian	
Saale Glaciation	High Lodge		
Hoxnian Interglacial	Acheulian	Clactonian	
Elster Glaciation			
Cromerian Interglacial			
Pre-Cromer Cold phases			

TABLE I

IN EUROPE

Sea Levels & Thames Terraces, &c.	Animals in Europe	Dates in years (conventional)
Younger Loess	Elephas primigenius · Woolly Rhinoceros · Reindeer	
7·5 metres Thames 25′ Terrace		
18 metres Thames 50′ Terrace? Older Loess		EEMIAN (90,000 B.C.)
32 metres Thames 100′ Terrace	Elephas antiquus	HOXNIAN (200,000 B.C.)
60 metres	Elephas meridionalis	

PLEISTOCENE CULTURES

South Africa

	Cores	Flakes	Blades
RECENT		Levalloisian technique surviving	Later Stone-Age Culture
UPPER PLEISTOCENE		Sangoan Culture Fauresmith Culture (Micoquian with Levalloisian) Stellenbosch continued with Micoquian Types	Solutrean-like Laurel-Leaf Culture (Still-Bay)
MIDDLE PLEISTOCENE		Stellenbosch (Acheulean with Proto-Levalloisian) Early Stellenbosch	
LOWER PLEISTOCENE		Pre-Stellenbosch Pebble and Flake Industries	

TABLE II

East Africa

Cores	Flakes	Blades
	Neolithic Cultures	
		Blade Cultures with Microliths & Pottery (Elmenteitan, Wilton)
	Still Bay Culture	African Aurignacian (Kenya Capsian)
	Sangoan	
Hand-Axes with Levalloisian flakes	Sangoan	Proto-Aurignacian (Basal, Kenya Capsian)
Chelles-Acheulean		
Oldowan		

Dates in Years B.C. according to C14 Method	Geological Stages		Movement of Shoreline[1] in Baltic Area & Stages of Baltic Sea
300			Mya Limnaea Sea Shoreline raised
2,000			Shoreline lowered
3,000		FLANDRIAN (Post Glacial)	Litorina Sea
5,000			Shoreline raised
5,600			
			Ancylus Lake Shoreline lowered
6,800	Scandinavian Ice divides at Ragunda		Yoldia Sea Shoreline raised
7,800	Scottish Valley Glaciation		
8,300		LATE WEICHSELIAN (Late Glacial)	
9,000			Baltic Ice Lake Shoreline raised
10,000			
14,000	Scottish Re-Advance		

[1] For complexities of this movement see text page 11. There is a raised beach in Sea. The land of the southern part of the North Sea tended to sink as Scandinavia rose, deep maritime deposits.

TABLE III

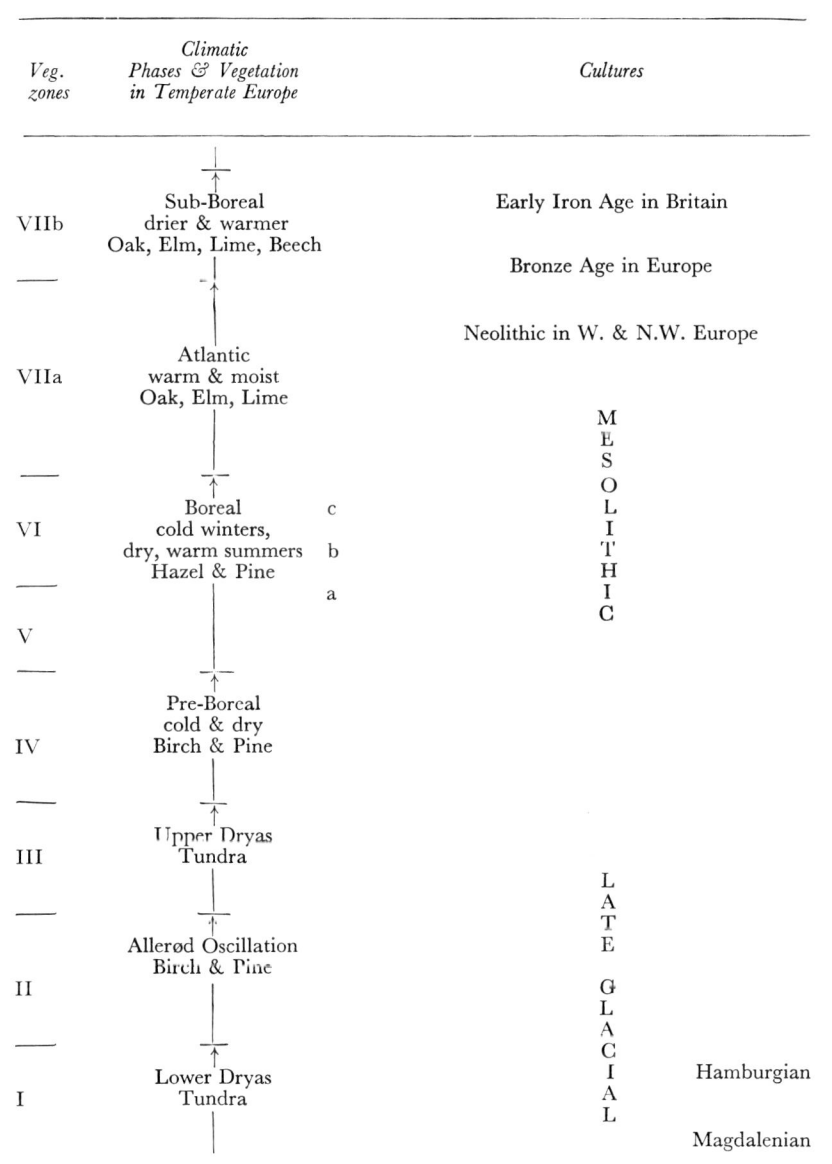

AND WEST EUROPE

Veg. zones	Climatic Phases & Vegetation in Temperate Europe		Cultures
VIIb	Sub-Boreal drier & warmer Oak, Elm, Lime, Beech		Early Iron Age in Britain Bronze Age in Europe
VIIa	Atlantic warm & moist Oak, Elm, Lime		Neolithic in W. & N.W. Europe M E S
VI	Boreal cold winters, dry, warm summers Hazel & Pine	c b a	O L I T H I C
V			
IV	Pre-Boreal cold & dry Birch & Pine		
III	Upper Dryas Tundra		L A T
II	Allerød Oscillation Birch & Pine		E G L A
I	Lower Dryas Tundra		C I Hamburgian A L Magdalenian

Scotland, N. England and N.E. Ireland corresponding to a high level of the Litorina Early Bronze Age remains of the S.E. English coast for example becoming buried under